Oman

Front cover: an early-morning
view of Mutrah, Muscat

Right: ornate street decoration

Nakhal Fort • A soaring structure in the Western Hajar Mountains *(page 50)*

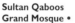

Sultan Qaboos Grand Mosque • A beautifully designed and decorated contemporary mosque with a capacity for 20,000 worshippers *(page 39)*

Al Hoota Cave • Spectacular underground formations *(page 45)*

Bait al Baranda • This excellent museum traces Muscat's history *(page 33)*

Dhow cruise • Enjoy tranquil bays and stunning views *(page 79)*

Museum of the Frankincense Land • A fascinating and fragrant history *(page 68)*

Ras al Jinz Turtle Reserve • Nesting site of endangered green turtles *(page 62)*

Sumhuram • The site of an ancient port in a beautiful setting on the banks of Khawr Rawri creek *(page 72)*

Mutrah Corniche and Souq • The exotic sights, sounds and smells of an authentic Arabian souq *(page 33)*

Nizwa Fort • A majestic fort with excellent views *(page 42)*

A PERFECT DAY

8.00am Breakfast

Join the power-walkers and joggers for an early-morning stroll along the quiet beach at Shati al Qurm, followed by a well-deserved outdoor breakfast at D'Arcy's in Jawaharat a'Shati Complex.

12 noon Coastal drive

Drive along the sweeping corniche and through the Muscat Gate into Old Muscat. Admire the facade of the Sultan's Al Alam Palace and take in the latest art exhibition at Bait Muzna Gallery.

11.00am Local history

Head for Mutrah and spend an hour at Bait al Baranda, a fascinating history museum. Have a hot drink at the Kargeen Caffe before moving on.

1.30pm Scenic lunch

Drive down the coast to the world-famous Al Bustan Palace Hotel for a superb buffet lunch. The Al Khiran Terrace restaurant offers indoor or outdoor dining with stunning views along the coast, and features 'live cooking stations' for personal freshly cooked dishes.

9.30am A mosque visit

Visit the Sultan Qaboos Grand Mosque for a look around this beautifully constructed and exquisitely decorated building, one of the most famous in Arabia. Women must remember to take a scarf to cover their heads.

IN MUSCAT

6.30pm A short stroll and an aperitif

Disembark and walk along the Corniche for early-evening drinks on the tiny top-floor terrace of the Marina Hotel. Enjoy fabulous views along Mutrah Corniche to the fort and beyond.

10.00pm Late-night jazz

Take a taxi back through town to the Park Inn at Al Khuwayr for some late-evening live jazz or lounge music at its laidback Sama Terrazza rooftop bar. Enjoy extensive night-time views towards the Sultan Qaboos Grand Mosque.

4.00pm Dhow cruise

Return to Mutrah Corniche to board a pre-booked sunset dhow cruise. Glide out of the harbour and along the coast into the bay of Old Muscat, often accompanied by dolphins, and take in views of the Sultan's Palace and the Portuguese forts of Al Mirani and Al Jalali.

8.00pm Dinner with a view

Reserve a table at La Brasserie, next door to the Marina Hotel, for exquisite French cuisine specialising in fish dishes. This small restaurant is spread over three floors, with the upper terrace having great views across the harbour and fish market.

26

36

48

CONTENTS

82

38

97

INTRODUCTION

Oman's potential as a tourist destination is still unfolding, but all the right ingredients are here: unspoilt landscapes, wonderful beaches, a rich culture and friendly people. Oman occupies the southeastern corner of the Arabian peninsula, straddling the Tropic of Cancer along the coast of the Indian Ocean and the Arabian Gulf. It has land borders with the UAE, Saudi Arabia and Yemen, and an area of just over 300,000 sq km (115,800 sq miles), making it slightly larger than Italy. Figures from the December 2010 census show a total population of 2,694,094, of which almost 2 million are Omani citizens and the rest (27 percent) are expats who have taken the opportunity to live and work in one of the safest and most stable Middle Eastern countries. Some 60 percent of the population live either in Muscat or along the Batinah coast, enjoying almost year-round sunshine.

Varied landscapes

One of your first impressions of Oman will be the vast stretches of colourful flowers that line the sweeping highways. Armies of imported workers tend the millions of petunias, marigolds, bougainvillea and oleander that offer pleasant urban driving. Beyond the city limits is a good network of coastal roads giving access to the cooler mountainous interior. Ample groundwater flows from these mountains providing 90 percent of requirements, distributed through the ancient system of *falaj* water channels, numbering around 40,000 – the longest of which is almost 10km (6 miles).

More than 2,100km (1,300 miles) of coastline stretch from the strategically important Strait of Hormuz, along the Gulf

Out for a stroll in Rustaq

Frankincense

There are over 300 types of incense trees, but the best-quality frankincense comes from the tree *Boswellia sacra*, known as silver frankincense. It grows abundantly in the Dhofar region, as does myrrh, of which *Commiphora myrrha* produces the best quality.

of Oman and Indian Ocean, to the Gulf of Aden in the south. Around the Musandam peninsula in the north and the province of Dhofar in the south, the coast is lined with steep, rugged cliffs, interspersed with small sandy bays. Between them is a gentler coastal stretch of shallow bays and sandy beaches, which attract a variety of wildlife, including the endangered green turtle which nests here. In Dhofar, a quirk of nature turns an otherwise searing summer coastline into a cool, misty rain-soaked landscape as the *khareef* monsoon brushes the Arabian peninsula at this one spot between June and September.

The Hajar Mountains stretch from the border with the UAE for some 500km (310 miles) down to Sur, rising to over 3,000m (9,800ft) in the Jabal Akhdar (Green Mountain) massif at the centre of the range. The verdant mountaintops and deep wooded valleys shelter a rich variety of flora and fauna.

The coastline between Muscat and the UAE border is the flat wide Batinah coast, dotted with impressive castles and large irrigated farms. South of Muscat towards Sur is a more rugged landscape of unbroken grey-sand beach, lapped by a gentle sea – yet the plain, never more than a kilometre wide, is still extensively cultivated, particularly with date plantations.

Beyond lies the stark, inhospitable landscape of Wahibah and the Empty Quarter deserts. But the desert is also a great preserver, with valuable oil reserves lying below the surface, waiting to be discovered. Petroleum Development Oman

(PDO) controls almost all of Oman's oil industry and employs the second-largest number of workers after the government.

Land of traditions

Modern Oman is embracing responsible tourism and is fast gaining a reputation as a destination for the discerning tourist wanting quality hotels, good food and adventure. The varied terrain and coastline offer unlimited adventures – 4x4 thrills in the gorges and deserts; mountain trekking; scuba-diving in clear seas teeming with fish; dhow sailing and plenty more besides. Oman's strategy has always been to target the luxury end of the tourist market, and it looks set to continue with the building of upmarket resorts such as The Wave project, a development worth US$805 million. But alongside high-end hotels and adventure travel, Oman also offers a taste of an older, pre-oil Arabia in its souqs and villages.

The exquisite beach at Salalah

Nizwa livestock market

Everyday life in Oman is still very traditional in many respects. The Omanis succeed in mixing modern life with established social traditions, taking delight in their culture and heritage, and recognising the importance of preserving them. Visiting the local souqs, tourists are often thrilled to buy the fragrant resin 'frankincense', obtained from trees that can still be seen growing in Dhofar. By doing so they continue a tradition going back thousands of years to the fabled Queen of Sheba, who travelled along the old trade routes and traded with the Egyptians. Despite its modern facilities, attending the Friday livestock market at Nizwa is like stepping back in time. Women in burqas watch the bustling crowd of men amidst heated negotiations, much as they have done for hundreds of years. As they depart in modern pickups and 4x4s, the recent change in their lives is obvious, but Omanis seem capable of handling this rapid transformation in a controlled way that protects their heritage and identity.

Islam in Oman

Most Omanis follow Ibadism, a particular brand of Islam, distinct from the Shia or Sunni forms, which has played a crucial role in the country's history. As in much of the Islamic world, Islam introduced a new and fervent intellectual debate into people's lives, centring on God's law and the organisation of society. This was especially true of Ibadism in Oman, and it was to produce an extensive Omani literature, particularly rich in law and history.

Islam, meaning 'submission', shapes the principles of government and permeates all aspects of believers' public and private lives, laying down rules for everyday conduct and social relationships. The faithful express their belief without self-consciousness wherever they happen to be, whether at home, in the street or in the mosque, in the five daily prayers.

The people of the coast of Oman and the Emirates have been exposed to a great deal of foreign influence, whether as seafarers along the coasts of India and East Africa, or at home where foreign trading communities have grown up. This has led them to tolerate religious differences, but without abandoning their own traditions and beliefs. The influential 'Lawati' Shia Muslims (also known as Khoja or Latyani), for example, arrived from northern India around 400 years ago. Their tight-knit community prospered on the trade of incense, jewellery and textiles, and is still centred on the beautiful mosque and minaret beside Mutrah Souq.

Most tourist itineraries will include a visit to the vast Sultan Qaboos Grand Mosque

Jirz axes

Some of the men wandering around Khasab still carry the traditional small axe known as a *jirz*. Used since ancient times, it is both a useful tool and a walking stick, with the diminutive axehead often embellished with engravings or inlaid brass.

Oil workers in Muscat

in Muscat, the only mosque in Oman that non-Muslims are permitted to visit.

Building a future

Oil wealth arrived late in Oman compared with Saudi Arabia and the UAE, but it has been put to good use in the past four decades by Sultan Qaboos, who has steered the country through rapid but controlled development. This is now a modern nation, strong and respected by its neighbours. As well as exporting large quantities of its own oil, Oman's unique position puts it in control of more than half the world's oil supply, which passes through the strategically important Strait of Hormuz. Like Dubai and Abu Dhabi, Oman has to perform a delicate balancing act between rapid growth from unsustainable oil revenues, and diversifying into non-oil-based industries, including sustainable tourism.

Under the leadership of Sultan Qaboos, an ambitious programme of education and training is geared to the long-term aim of putting Omani people into many of the jobs currently filled by foreigners. This 'Omanisation' will not only create a sustainable future for the country, but will further enhance Oman's reputation for quality and innovation, whilst retaining the strong heritage and culture that makes it unique. The Oman brand has a bright future.

A BRIEF HISTORY

Oman's unique position between Africa and Asia places it at the centre of human development and the spread of early civilisation. Trade contacts with ancient Egypt, Mesopotamia and the Indus Valley highlight the importance of this location, which has been a blessing and a hindrance throughout its history. Persian dominance dictated Oman's subsidiary role for more than 2,000 years, and then came the Portuguese, who dominated international trade in the Gulf and Indian Ocean for over a century. After the expulsion of the Portuguese in the 17th century, Oman controlled its own destiny, even though coastal Muscat and interior Nizwa were often battling for supremacy. Islam, of course, has played a crucial role in the country's history. But the speed and scale of change brought about by the discovery of oil in the Arabian Gulf in the 1950s was unprecedented in world history.

Prehistory

Recent archaeological explorations of Oman have revealed a rich and varied ancient history. Archaeological surveys indicate a constantly changing mosaic of coastal and inland settlements, but many of the earliest sites lie along the shores of the Gulf of Oman. The area around Taqah in Dhofar is particularly rich in fossils, especially of early primates from around 30 million years ago,

Map of the Arabian peninsula, c.1575

when Arabia was connected to Africa. Dating is difficult, but it could indicate that Arabia was more important in primate development than previously thought. Many sites in southern Arabia had a climate suitable for human settlement. Evidence of early migration from Africa around 125,000 years ago has been found near Mudayy (about 80km/50 miles inland from Mughsayl) in Dhofar.

Until about 16,000 years ago, when sea levels began to rise, the area now occupied by the Gulf would have formed a river valley extending as far as the Strait of Hormuz. The shoreline would have been distant from its present location and 100–150m (330–490ft) lower than the present day average sea level. When the level began to rise it created a variety of coastal landscapes, including the fjord-like coastline of the Musandam peninsula, the plain of the Batinah and the steep cliffs extending from north of Muscat south past

The *falaj* water system

The most precious commodity for any settlement in Arabia is water. It is unclear whether the *falaj* system, an ingenious ancient irrigation system, originated in Arabia or Persia. The history of the *falaj* (plural *aflaj*) began around 3,000 years ago, when underground channels were dug by hand to transport water from the mountains to villages and farmland from mother wells dug into the water table. Vertical shafts allow ventilation and the removal of silt and stones carried down the channel. In Oman the best ancient examples are found on the lower slopes around Jabal al Akhdar. Because *aflaj* were so vital in these inhospitable areas they were often protected by watchtowers, as an entire settlement such as Nizwa could quickly be defeated by cutting off its water supply. The job of digging and repairing the *falaj* is highly skilled and traditionally a specialisation of Oman's Awamir tribe, who have the nerve and agility required to work underground in small tunnels full of dust.

A *falaj* water channel

Ras al Hadd. These varied marine habitats afforded a glut of easily obtained fish and shellfish. Mangroves attracted birdlife which could be hunted, and adjacent inland areas supported gazelle and, later on, grazing for sheep, goats and cattle. The earliest manmade objects, dating as far back as the 5th millennium BC, have been unearthed at coastal settlements such as Ras al Hamra near Qurm. Excavation of 'shell middens' here has revealed the ground plan of small groups of circular buildings, indicated by stone foundations or arrangements of post-holes. Other finds, such as those at the Neolithic sites of Ras al Jinz and Sur, show that the inhabitants were adept at making stone tools and artefacts.

Early civilisations

The Mesopotamian civilisation at Ur in Sumeria (now southern Iraq) lacked metal ores such as copper, which they imported from the Wadi Jizzi region of Oman, inland from

القرآن... (Arabic text at top of illustration)

A 13th-century illustration of a merchant's dhow

Sohar. A clay tablet found at Ur describes an amount equating to 20 tonnes of copper arriving from 'Magan' (northern Oman). Copper smelted around Arja, Beidha and Lusayl could easily be carried down Wadi Jizzi to the port at Sohar before being transported around the Gulf. However, a more direct route ran via Buraymi Oasis and Umm An Nar, the old trading island off the coast of Abu Dhabi. During the so-called Umm An Nar period (2,600–2,000BC), the copper was taken along the Gulf coast to ancient Dilmun (Bahrain) and thence to the Sumerian cities.

As imported iron replaced copper through the 1st millennium BC, the old copper-working sites of Oman were abandoned. Instead, gold, cornelian, spices, animal hides and oils were carried along the trade routes. Around this time the domestication of the camel improved desert trade and communication. The invention of the *falaj* system also increased food production and led to a rise in population in these well-watered places at the base of the Hajar Mountains.

Meanwhile in Dhofar, the controlled cultivation and distribution of aromatic gum resins, particularly frankincense, can be dated back as far as 1,000BC. Under the control of the Queen of Sheba, great desert cities like Ubar and the port at Sumhuram sent these precious goods to the temples of ancient Egypt. But the clever Omani merchants had also mastered the seasonal monsoon winds and were trading with Southeast Asia and East Africa, importing spices, silk, ivory, animal skins and slaves.

From the 6th century BC, the dominant power was Persia, with an empire extending to Egypt and India. The Persians controlled Sohar, which for most of its history was far more important than Muscat. By the time of Greek and then Roman dominance, trade from Ethiopia, southwest Arabia and India into the Near East and Mediterranean was in full swing, much of it by camel caravan along the great land routes of the Arabian peninsula. From the 3rd century BC the region fell under Greek influence as they pushed eastwards through Asia. By 250BC the Parthians (from northeastern Iran) controlled all sea trade (including ports in Oman) and established themselves as the middle men in the development of the silk trade from China, both overland and by sea. During the Sassanid rule of Persia in the 5th century sea trade was back in the hands of Persian seamen, who successfully fought both the Romans and the Arabs for regional control.

Boswellia, the tree which yields frankincense resin, c. AD990

Arrival of Islam

The year AD570 is highly significant in Oman's history. It is the year the prophet Muhammad was born in Mecca (in Saudi Arabia), and the year the great dam at Marib (in Yemen) finally collapsed – Marib was the capital of the Kingdom of Sheba,

Jewel of Muscat

A major feat of engineering was the recent reconstruction of a 9th-century Arab sailing ship using traditional methods at Qantab boatyard near Muscat. Between February and July 2010, an Omani crew successfully sailed the 18m (59ft) *Jewel of Muscat* across the Indian Ocean to Singapore, retracing part of the historic maritime trade route between Arabia and the Far East.

which controlled the trade of frankincense from Dhofar. The abandonment of Marib by the Azd tribes resulted in the gradual migration – of the Azdi Umani tribe in particular – along the incense trade route into Oman. They settled at the port of Qalhat near Sur and under their leader, Malik Bin Fahim al Azd, ousted the occupying Sassanians and asserted control over eastern trade with India.

Islam spread along the established desert trade routes and is said to have been introduced into Oman during the lifetime of the Prophet Muhammad. The Prophet sent early Islamic emissaries from Medina to all the tribes and settlements of Arabia. The one he sent to Oman was the general Amr Ibn al As. Though Amr targeted the flourishing Persian port and capital of Sohar on the Omani coast, it was the Arab tribal ruling family, the Al Jalenda, and not the Persian governor, who accepted his message. There are several mosques in Oman claiming to exist from the lifetime of the Prophet, including the Al Midhamr mosque at Samail, between Nizwa and Muscat. Even though they have been rebuilt many times, all of these early mosques lie on important pre-Islamic trade routes.

Within the first few decades of Islam, the tribes chose to follow the Ibadi school (distinct from Sunni or Shia), founded by Jabir Ibn Zaid al Azdi from Nizwa. It remains the dominant form of Islam in Oman today. Inter-Islamic conflicts ended with a period of relative peace at the beginning of the 9th century which lasted more than 300 years.

Maritime trade

In medieval times, the main port of Sohar prospered greatly under the Abbasid caliphs of Baghdad, as its ships traded around the Indian Ocean and further east to China. Sohar's intrepid sailors are said to have inspired the legend of Sindbad. Around 1330 the Muslim traveller Ibn Battuta described Muscat as 'a small place' when compared to the greatness of Sohar and Qalhat, another prosperous port near Sur. On his way overland to Mecca he stopped at Nizwa, capital of the interior, which he reports as being under the control of tribal kings known as the Bani Nabhan, who ruled for almost three centuries, while the coast was back under Persian rule. Since then, control of the country has been a constant tussle between a coastal hereditary sultan and an interior elected imam.

Portuguese navigators sailed around the Indian Ocean in the early 16th century, making great use of Oman's existing

The *Jewel of Muscat*

seafaring knowledge. They occupied Muscat and defended it with the forts that can still be seen today. After almost 150 years the Portuguese were eventually expelled by Sultan Ibn Saif al Ya'arubi, who also seized Portuguese territories in East Africa and developed a lucrative slave trade.

The Omani Empire

Following internal conflict, the country was united by Ahmed Ibn Said who started the Al Bu Said dynasty, which has endured to this day. Through a succession of largely popular rulers, Oman increased its sea trade by attacking and occupying overseas territories in the Gulf and East Africa until Zanzibar became the centre of Oman's slave trade. Through the 1830s Sultan Said Bin Sultan extended the empire to its greatest size and made Zanzibar his capital. Agreements were concluded with European powers, and Oman became the first Arab country to establish diplomatic relations with the USA in 1833. But fortunes reversed when the British banned slavery in the same year, after which Oman's economy collapsed.

British support of the Al Bu Said rulers angered many of the nearby Gulf States which were constantly at war with the Al Bu Said over interior territories. British ships came under threat until they concluded a truce with all the local coastal tribes, declaring them the 'Trucial States'. The development of the steamship and opening of the Suez Canal in 1869 left Oman isolated, as larger vessels could bypass its ports and travel directly to India from the Red Sea.

Sultan Seyyid Said abolished the slave trade in Oman in 1845

Special Air Service Regiment on camel patrol, 1960

Creation of modern Oman

Internal dissatisfaction by followers of the imam in Nizwa (supported by the Saudis) led to British support of the Al Bu Said rulers in Muscat until the Treaty of Seeb in 1920, which divided control between the 'Imam of the Muslims' and the 'Sultan of Muscat and Oman'. New tribal alliances were formed by Sultan Said Bin Taimur in 1955, when he drove from Dhofar across the desert to Nizwa to assert control, protect Oman's oil interests and force the retreat of the imam. He continued on to Buraymi in order to strike a deal with the Abu Dhabi ruler that split Buraymi/Al Ain, straddling the Oman/UAE border, in half. Further skirmishes caused uncertainty to oil prospecting in the Buraymi region, leading to the 'Jabal Akhdar Incidents' which finally ended resistance to the Sultan's rule, not least with bombing raids by Britain's RAF *(see page 44)*. Oman changed for ever when oil was finally struck at the Natih Field in 1963.

In the mid-1960s the separatist movement to oust the British from Aden spilled over from South Yemen and became known as the Dhofar Mutiny in Oman. It was eventually put down after a decade with help from Britain's SAS.

When he took over from his father in 1970 Sultan Qaboos embarked on a much-needed modernisation programme. When he came to power there were only three schools, two graded roads and one hospital in the whole country, no newspapers, radio or television, and no civil service. Over the last 40 years, Oman has been transformed, through oil and gas earnings, into a land with public electricity and water, even in remote villages, and hospitals, schools and universities around the country. The average life expectancy has risen from 47 to over 70. Diverse tribal groups separated by hundreds of kilometres have now been connected by a network of good roads, creating a greater sense of national unity.

Omani at the Sultan Qaboos Grand Mosque

The unrest that swept across the Arab world in early 2011 encouraged demonstrations in Sohar against unemployment and representation, rather than against Sultan Qaboos himself.

The rapid progress made over the last decades is there for all to see. Oman is now a modern Arab country, yet one that still retains it own traditions and identity.

Historical landmarks

5,000BC Early human settlements along the coast.

2,500BC Copper trade from 'Magan' to Mesopotamia.

1,000BC *Falaj* system of underground water channels developed; frankincense traded from Dhofar to ancient Egypt.

6th century BC Persian Empire controls the region.

3rd century BC Greek influence on Asian trade, followed by Romans.

3rd–6th century AD Migration of Azd tribe from Marib into Oman.

AD570 Birth of Prophet Muhammad and final destruction of Marib Dam.

628 Islam arrives in Oman. First mosque built at Samail.

9th century Sohar prospers under control of the Abassid caliphate in Baghdad.

1330 Arab geographer and writer Ibn Battuta travels through Oman.

1507 Portuguese control the major ports.

1650 Expulsion of Portuguese by Sultan Ibn Saif al Ya'arubi.

1744 Ahmed Ibn Said starts the Al Bu Said dynasty.

1830s Greatest extent of Omani Empire with its capital at Zanzibar.

1853 'Trucial States' peace treaty concluded with the British.

1920 British support for Al Bu Said ruler after the Treaty of Seeb.

1925 First geological survey in the search for oil.

1946 Wilfred Thesiger leaves Dhofar to cross the Empty Quarter desert.

1950 Formation of the Trucial Oman Scouts, a defence force led by British officers.

1955 Sultan Said Bin Taimur reunites 'Oman and Muscat' with Nizwa.

1963 Oil first discovered at the Natih Field.

1963 Start of the Dhofar Mutiny.

1970 Sultan Qaboos takes control of Oman from his father Sultan Said.

1981 Oman is founder member of the GCC (Gulf Co-operation Council) comprising Saudi Arabia, Kuwait, the UAE, Bahrain, Qatar and Oman.

2001 The Sultan Qaboos Grand Mosque opens in Muscat.

2010 Oman successfully hosts the Asian Beach Games.

2011 Minor demonstrations in Sohar following general unrest in the Middle East.

WHERE TO GO

Almost all visits will start and end in the Omani capital, Muscat, either at the airport or the harbour. Muscat makes a good base for exploring the north: the mountainous interior around Nizwa, the flat Batinah coast, and the rugged east coast to Sur. Dhofar and Musandam are the southern and northern extremities of the country, easily reached by internal flights from Muscat or lengthy road trips. As the roads are continually upgraded, there are more routes and possible circuits for non 4x4 vehicles. Visitors from the UAE can drive directly into Musandam or choose to fly or drive into Muscat.

MUSCAT

The tranquil Old Town of **Muscat** clings to a small natural harbour, its hidden inlets legendary for their forts, palaces and souqs. In the neighbouring bay, less than 3km (2 miles) along the coast road, is the port of Mutrah, where bustling markets echo with the calls of traders selling their fish, frankincense and fine silks. Old Muscat is a quiet place to wander, retaining many of its traditional houses and mosques. Although opportunities for tourism abound in Mutrah, the port caters primarily for trade and local fishermen. But the corniche has a few hidden gems leading from it.

Old Muscat and Mutrah are just fragments of modern Muscat. Since the 1970s, the city has grown with the help of oil money, and new business and office districts have sprouted in all directions. Modern highways and flyovers cut through a dramatic topography, leading from one tranquil district to the

The golden dome of the Sultan Qaboos Grand Mosque

Al Alam Palace

next up the coast towards Seeb International Airport and into the neighbouring valleys. The main commercial and residential development has occured in Ruwi, the Central Business District; Qurm is where the shopping complexes are concentrated; Medinat Qaboos is a mainly residential area; and Al Khuwayr is a district of ministerial buildings and embassies.

Old Muscat

Although Muscat's foundation dates from the 1st century AD, the town didn't gain recognition until the 14th and 15th centuries, when it attracted traders. In the 16th century it drew the Portuguese, who developed Muscat as their principal naval base and strengthened its defences – until 1650 when they were ousted by an Omani force.

The approach to the old walled city is via the coast road which leads uphill to the Gateway. This reconstructed entranceway spanning the main road houses the **Muscat Gate**

Museum (Sat–Thur 9.30am–1.30pm, 4.30–7pm; free; tel: 9932 8754), a room full of information panels on Omani history and traditions.

Old Muscat is home to some fabulous old houses and mosques and is easily viewed on foot. In the heart of its winding streets one of the historic houses has been converted into a fine museum. **Bait al Zubair** (Sat–Thur 9.30am–1pm, 4–7pm; charge; no photography; tel: 2473 6688; www. baitalzubairmuseum.com) in Al Saidiya Street houses impressive displays and collections. The sections on women's jewellery, adornment and clothing are particularly informative, with superb examples. Differences in regional dress for men are also explained, and the collection of old *khanjars* (Omani daggers), some made entirely of gold, is worth a look. The latest addition is a series of scaled models of famous forts around the country. The comfortable coffee shop is in another restored old house, and the extensive souvenir shop offers a range of books and upmarket gifts, such as frankincense-scented candles, quality replicas of the museum's jewellery and the full range of Amouage perfumes. Space around the Bait al Zubair is used for temporary art exhibitions and displays.

Across the road, the former royal residence of Sultan Qaboos's aunt Muzna has been converted into the sleek **Bait Muzna Gallery** (9.30am–7pm; free; tel: 2473 9204; www.baitmuznagallery.com), an attractive setting for high-quality Omani-inspired art and design, with the occasional poetry reading or gallery talk (check website for details).

Sailors' calling card

Some visiting sailors painted their ship's names along the craggy outcrops of Muscat Bay, the most obvious of which is HMS *Falmouth*. Rather than seeing it as graffiti, the previous sultan called it his great open-air visitors' book.

Several fine 18th-century buildings have served as embassies and consulates. Among those still standing is the Bait Fransa, the residence of French consuls until 1920, now the **Omani-French Museum** (Sat–Thur 9am–1pm; charge; tel: 2473 6613), commemorating Oman's historical links with France. French ships carrying spices and sugar from the Indian Ocean had called at Muscat since the 17th century, and in the 19th century trade links intensified.

C ▶ The centrepiece of Old Muscat is the **Al Alam Palace**. The 1970s architecture of the official Sultan's residence clashes somewhat with the surrounding buildings. The story-book facade can be viewed through the gates at the end of the pedestrianised street. The roof seems to be held up by a series of giant golf tees painted in blue and gold. The other side of the palace looks out over the narrow bay, protected by two hilltop forts, both legacies of Portuguese control in the 16th century. Access to the bay is along a road that passes the blue and white Al Khawr mosque. Towering above it is the western fort of **Al Mirani**, completed in 1587. The eastern fort on the other side of the palace, **Al Jalali**, completed in 1588, was formerly the city jail. Neither fort is open to the public.

At the far end of the bay are the small dockyards for

Royal naval sailing yacht, *Zinat al Bihar*

the magnificent Royal Navy of Oman sail training vesse! *Shabab Oman* and yacht *Zinat al Bihar* that sail around the world promoting Omani seamanship.

South of Old Muscat

The road south from Old Muscat skirts around the harbours of Sidab and Haramil until it drops down to Marina Bander Ar Raw-dah, home of the Marine

The cavernous lobby of the Al Bustan Palace Hotel

Fisheries and Science Centre and its **Aquarium** (Sat–Wed 8am–2.30pm, Thur 8am–1pm, Fri 3–7pm; free; tel: 2473 6449). A large tank at one end is given over to some moray eels, including an impressive brown and white honeycomb and several silver sweetlips. At the other end are some green sea turtles that look much happier wheeling around under-water than lumbering up the beach to lay eggs. Other high-lights are some intriguing remoras and the curiously beautiful Picasso triggerfish.

Continue along the same road to the roundabout with a full-size wooden boat in the centre. This is the *Sohar*, a repli-ca of a 9th-century dhow built for British adventurer Tim Severin's expedition to retrace the sea journey of the legend-ary Omani sailor Sindbad *(see page 59)*.

Beyond the roundabout, standing majestically in its own bay is the **Al Bustan Palace Hotel**. Luxuriously elegant fol-lowing its two-year modernisation, it is regularly voted one of the top hotels in the Middle East, and is a real treat for non-resident visitors to look around. Sadly this is not the case for the more distant Shangri-La Barr al Jissah Resort, which discourages casual visitors by making it impossible to park anywhere nearby, so best to get dropped off by taxi.

Between the two resorts is the excellent **Oman Dive Centre**, situated in its own idyllic shallow inlet, and the picturesque fishing village of **Qantab**, which still retains much of its local flavour.

Mutrah

Mutrah and Old Muscat are connected by a coastal road that twists around jagged mountains and bays, continually providing new vistas. From the frantic early-morning activity of the fish market to the laidback atmosphere of an evening stroll around the souq, the wide expanse of Mutrah harbour is always busy and full of life. Your first stop should be the **fish market**, a lively spectacle. Despite sometimes being outnumbered by tourists, the fish-sellers always seem happy to

The C38 trail

This trek quickly transports you from the bustling corniche into remarkably quiet and rugged terrain. Marked by yellow/white/red-painted signs, the 90-minute trail climbs a total of 150m (490ft) before returning to sea level at Mutrah. The walk begins in Riyam Park – pick up the coloured markers in the parking area. From behind the small mosque, follow the stone steps and rusty pipeline to the top of the hill. The views from the high ground are splendid. Beyond the abandoned village the trail then descends a narrow wadi bed with smooth and slippery stones, to Mutrah. Good walking boots, water and a hat are essential. Do not trek alone and take great care on this isolated but worthwhile route. If starting from Mutrah, turn right off the corniche along Way 805 with Bank Muscat on the corner. Go straight over the crossroads signposted 'Wadi Khalfan St' until you see a large concrete dam. Follow a path into a cemetery on the right and ascend from here.

Mutrah fish market

pose for photos. Early arrival is advisable, as it gets less busy
through the day. On the other side of 'Fish' roundabout (the
start of the corniche) is the **Bait al Baranda** (Sat–Thur
9am–1pm, 4–6pm; charge; tel: 2471 4262), 'the house with
the veranda' museum covering the history of Muscat and
Oman – from geology, prehistory and early man through to
Islam, colonisation and the modern state. Explanations are
informed, concise and well illustrated.

Walking along **Mutrah Corniche**, with the sea on one side
and the backdrop of old buildings and mountains on the
other, is one of Muscat's great pleasures. Old merchants'
houses, gold shops and fruit-juice shops line the roadway
around the main souq entrance, overlooked by the tiny and
wonderfully laidback Al Cornish café. Though modern (concrete booths replaced the original palm structures in the
1970s), the narrow lanes of the **Mutrah Souq**, imbued with
the scent of frankincense and sandalwood, bustle with

traders, money-changers and shoppers eager to do business. The souq, one of the most authentic in Arabia, has specialist sections for gold, perfumes, silk, leather, jewellery and countless other goods, punctuated by *halwa* (sweetmeat) sellers and coffee shops. Unlike many other Middle Eastern cities, there is little hassle and you will always be treated courteously. Free public toilets are located beside the main souq entrance.

Be sure to observe the 'Residents Only' notices asking tourists not to visit the nearby **Lawatiya quarter**, dominated by the beautiful blue and white decorated Lawati mosque, which houses a Shia sect of the same name. Their residential area is walled and off-limits to outsiders.

Traditional gold work at the National Museum, Ruwi

The as yet unrestored **Mutrah Fort** dominates the end of the first section of Corniche. You can continue the 3km (2-mile) coast walk to the Gateway into Old Muscat, but it takes about an hour and can get very hot.

Riyam Park and **Kalbuh Park** (Sat–Wed 4–11pm, Thur–Fri and public hols 9am–noon; free) are popular for a sunset stroll. For the fit and adventurous there is even a short hike that completes a circuit from Riyam Park back to Mutrah through the rough mountain terrain (*see box, page 32*).

Ruwi

Separated from the Mutrah Corniche by low mountains is the Mutrah (or Central) Business District (MBD or CBD), developed in the 1970s and home to most of the banks, airlines and travel agencies. Apart from one or two museums worth visiting, the main reason to come to this area is the wide range of restaurants, mainly aimed at office workers.

> **Old runway**
>
> The main street of the Central Business District running down to the Clock Tower was, amazingly, the runway of Muscat's airport until 1973. The Sultan's Armed Forces Museum inside Bait al Falaj Fort was previously at the northern end of the runway.

To the north of the district, the small Bait al Falaj Fort, built in 1845, is now home to the **Sultan's Armed Forces Museum** (Sat–Wed 8am–1.30pm, Thur–Fri 9–11am, 3–6pm; charge; tel: 2431 2655; www.safmuseum.gov.om), which gives an interesting glimpse into Oman's military history. In the *falaj* garden are displays of tanks, armoured vehicles, aeroplanes, rockets, Exocet missiles, a navy ship and a bullet-proof Cadillac.

Ruwi proper lies across the dry wadi bed with the ONTC bus station and taxi stand at its centre. Behind the taxi stand is the modern Ruwi souq, full of electrical, optical and phone shops. Across Al Burj Street from the Al Falaj Hotel on A'Noor Street is the well-hidden **National Museum** (Sat–Wed 8am–1.30pm, Thur 9am–1pm, closed Fri; charge; tel: 2470 1289), sometimes now called the Heritage and Culture Museum. Highlights here include displays of the ancient copper trade *(see page 54)* and Bat Tombs near Ibri *(see page 48)*, the fabulous silver jewellery of Seyyida Salma, daughter of the Sultan of Oman and Zanzibar 1804–56, and superb 16th–18th-century vases from the Far East. The museum is expected to move to Old Muscat in 2013.

Qurm

This area is mostly made up of shopping centres and residences, but the landscape opens up around **Qurm Natural Park** (Sat–Wed 4–11pm, Thur–Fri and public holidays 9am–midnight; free), a recreational area and protected reserve of mangroves which spreads from the highway to the beach. The park is popular for family outings, with large grassy areas for picnics, playgrounds, food outlets, a lake, mock forts, and the adjoining Marah Land amusement park. Enter from the main gate on Al Qurm Street or from below Mumtaz Mahal restaurant near the open-air amphitheatre. At the southern edge of the park, in the **Children's Museum** (Sat–Wed 8am–1.30pm, Thur 9am–1pm and Mon afternoon 4–6pm; nominal charge; tel: 2460 5368), the whole family can investigate gravity, air movement, sound waves, whisper dishes, probability outcomes, the human body and many other games and puzzles. Lots of fun.

Young footballer, Qurm Park

Follow Sayh al Maleh Street from the Marah Land funfair towards the PDO (Petroleum Development Oman) oil facility at Mina al Fahl and turn right just before the main entrance gate no. 2 into a small car park. The white building is the **Oil & Gas Exhibition Centre** (Sat–Wed 7am–3.45pm, Thur 8am–noon; free; tel: 2467 7834; www.pdo.co.om), with hands-on displays, explanations of geology, exploration, extraction and transportation, and a neighbouring **Planetarium** (one-hour shows in English every Wed 7pm and Thur 10am; free admission, but bookings must be made at least 24 hours in advance; tel: 2467 5542; email: planetarium@pdo.co.om).

Running between the mangroves and the sandy beach, Al Shati Street (Qurm Beach Road) is a popular evening gathering place for promenading roadsters. The four restaurant/coffee shops here do great business and offer stunning views towards sunset. At the eastern end is the Crowne Plaza Hotel with its small private cove and beach, overlooked by the **Ras al Hamra** headland. A walled site here shows evidence of human occupation 6,000 years ago *(see page 17)*.

Shati al Qurm continues west along the beach to the relaxed and pleasant 'Oasis by the Sea' area of shops, cafés and restaurants, some with beach views and terraces. Across the road is the Jawaharat a'Shati Complex, where the **Oman Heritage Gallery** (Sat–Thur 10am–8pm; tel: 2469 6974) sells upmarket locally produced items on a non-profit basis. Near the Al Shati Plaza and next door to the Ramada Hotel, the **Omani Society of Fine Arts** (Sat–Wed 9.30am–1.30pm, 6–8.30pm; free; tel: 2469 4969) promotes art and photography appreciation.

Beach at Ras al Hamra

Madinat as Sultan Qaboos
Inland from Shati al Qurm across the main highway, the residential area of Madinat

Traditional henna hand art

as Sultan Qaboos has two museums of interest. Follow signs to the Press Club to reach the **Museum of Omani Heritage** (Sat–Thur 8am–1.30pm; charge; tel: 2460 0946), which gives an insight into traditional family life and Omani culture. The **Bait Adam Museum** (Sat–Thur 9am–1pm 4–7pm; charge; tel: 2460 5033; email: baitadam@omantel.net.om), signposted off Madinat as Sultan Qaboos Street, is a remarkable private collection of photographs, coins, currency and stamps. Oman's relations with Zanzibar and the USA are revealed through important documents. Meals for small groups can be arranged directly or through any of the major tour agencies.

Al Khuwayr

The **Natural History Museum** (Sat–Wed 8am–1.30pm, Thur 9am–1pm, Sun also 4–6pm; charge; tel: 2460 4957) in Al Khuwayr is one of the most engaging museums of its size and kind anywhere, but especially welcome in a country where good background information is still hard to come by. The main attraction is a gallery of stuffed animals showing the country's diversity of wildlife. In a separate building, the Whale and Dolphin Hall exhibits skeletons found along Oman's coast, including a sperm whale suspended from the ceiling. Nearer to the coast, the **Sayyid Faisal Bin Ali Museum** (Sat–Wed 8am–2pm; charge; tel: 2464 1650), named after a former Minister of Heritage and Culture, houses a fine collection of weapons and hosts visiting art exhibitions from around the world. Across the highway is the distinctively modern Az Zawawi mosque, beside which stands the **Ice-Skating Centre** (9am–10pm; tel: 2448 9492), which provides a welcome break from the heat. This whole area is rapidly expanding, with many new hotels and restaurants.

The highway towards the airport then passes through Bawshar roundabout to the enormous **Sultan Qaboos** **Grand Mosque** (open to non-Muslims, but no children under 12; Sat–Thur 8am–11am; free; tel: 2459 2417), a 'must' for all visitors and a unique opportunity to see inside an Omani mosque. This magnificent building, which opened in 2001, was constructed by the best craftsmen to celebrate the 30th anniversary of the Sultan's reign. It covers 40,000 sq m (over 430,000 sq ft), and its main minaret rises to a height of 91.5m (300ft). The expansive prayer hall accommodates 6,500

Sultan Qaboos Grand Mosque

worshippers below a stunning crystal chandelier and large dome, which is distinctively illuminated at night. The vast carpet, made in Iran, took over two years to make and features 28 different colours obtained from natural dyes. Visitors should wear long sleeves and trousers, and women must bring a headscarf.

The opening of the huge 'Muscat City Centre' shopping mall beyond the airport shows how far the city is expanding. Just after the start of the nearby road to Nizwa is the **Amouage Perfumery** (Sun–Thur 8.30–4.30; free; tel: 2453 4800; www. amouage.com), where you can learn about perfume production and sample the varieties. Amouage perfumes, which incorporate frankincense, rosewater and myrrh, were created in the 1980s, to try to revive Oman's perfume tradition. Noted for its beautiful packaging in silver bottles plated with 24-carat gold, Amouage is one of the most expensive perfumes in the

The glittering prayer hall of the Sultan Qaboos Grand Mosque

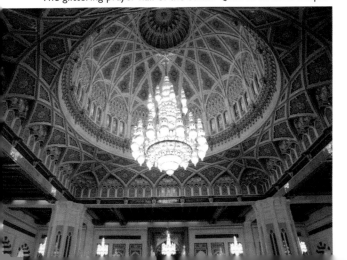

world, but the company has since launched a more affordable range.

The new Muscat Expressway opened in early 2011 runs 55km (35 miles) from Qurm to **Naseem Gardens** (Sat–Wed 4–11pm, Thur–Fri and public holidays 9am–midnight; free), a sprawling park on the way to Barka. The lakes, trees and formal gardens were opened in 1985, and a Japanese Garden was added in 2000. Together with Qurm Natural Park, it is the main focus of the annual Muscat Festival in January and February.

> **Amouage Gold**
>
> Amouage's heady signature fragrance, Gold, is often likened to the Hermès classic Calèche. Women's perfume bottles have tops shaped like a mosque dome, while men's take the form of *khanjar* daggers.

NIZWA AND THE MOUNTAINS

Former capital of a rival imam as recently as the 1950s, Nizwa and its inhabitants have always had a different outlook to Muscat. The people here look inwards to the mountainous Ad Dakhiliyah interior and the desert, rather than outwards from the coast. The whole region is a paradise for adventure-seekers – up, down and even inside the Hajar Mountains, with the desert not far away.

Muscat to Nizwa

Beyond Muscat International Airport, the main road to Nizwa enters the mountains at Ar Rusayl. A huge area to the north of this road, around Al Khawd, is destined to be the ambitious **Oman Botanic Garden** (due to open in 2012; www.oman-botanic-garden.org). The idea is to create a sustainable garden reserve, featuring some 1,200 plants covering eight different environments, all accessed by 'land train'.

Nizwa Fort

Towards Nizwa is **Samail**, a small but neat town, its square the site of the Al Midhamr mosque, said to be the oldest in Oman. It was built in 6AH (AD628) by Mazin bin Ghadouba, the first Omani convert to Islam.

Nizwa

Situated at the crossroads of ancient desert and mountain routes and blessed with a good water supply from the nearby mountains, **Nizwa** became a central hub linking the remote interior with the coast. This strategic position made it wealthy through trade, and for much of its history, Nizwa has been a powerful rival to Muscat and Sohar. Today it is the most popular tourist destination outside Muscat. Most coach tours stay for just a day, but to see Nizwa properly and to visit other interesting places in the interior requires two or three days. Exiting the main highway (which continues to Jabrin and Ibri), the road into Nizwa passes most of the hotels.

The imposing 400-year-old **Nizwa Fort** (Sat–Thur 9am–4pm, Fri 8–11am; charge) in the middle of town, has often needed to defend itself against invaders, particularly the Persians. Started in 1656 by Imam Sultan Ibn Saif Ya'arubi (who expelled the Portuguese), it was the main defensive stronghold of the town and residence of the *wali* (local governor) and his retinue. Leading from the internal courtyard is the 'Exhibits Hall', which has good explanations about local farming, the *falaj* system, crafts and a comprehensive timeline from prehistory. Climb up the impressive central tower for views over the town, market and surrounding date plantations. The outer courtyard has a small café, souvenir shop and toilets.

Just outside the main gateway is the **Omani Craftsman's House**, selling many local items. This road leads down to the tourist market of shops piled high with Bahla pots, decorated sea chests and colourful incense burners. Further along are the local markets for fruit and vegetables, meat and fish. The animal market *(see box below)* overlooks the wadi bed, which acts as a giant car park for most of the time.

Around Nizwa

The road to the famous forts of Bahla and Jabrin loops north along the foot of the Jabal al Akhdar Mountains. Almost immediately on the left after passing the 'Book' roundabout is

Nizwa livestock market

If possible, try to visit Nizwa on a Friday morning to witness the weekly animal market. The wadi car park and surrounding streets fill up from 6am as villagers arrive to sell their cows and goats. Owners walk the animals around a central ring, with potential buyers watching from both sides. A quick inspection or enquiry about an animal might lead to lengthier negotiations, conducted outside the parade ring. Dealings can get a bit heated, but generally it's all done in good spirit, and most locals seem happy for tourists to take photographs. Some of the larger cattle get a bit fed up with walking around and make an escape bid through the crowd, dragging the hapless owner with them. By 9am it is all winding down, as people drift away to buy other items at the adjacent 'car boot' sale which spreads along the wadi bed.

Livestock market, Nizwa

a small watchtower overlooking a large plain, said to be Caliph Harun Ar Rashid's camp during his battles for regional control in the late 8th century AD. Some 20km (12 miles) from Nizwa, the next turning is for **Tanuf**, a ruined village at the entrance to a gorge. The buildings were destroyed by RAF bombers when Sultan Bin Taimur asked for Britain's aid in suppressing local support for the Imamate revolution in the 1950s *(see page 23)*. Further into the gorge is Qayut village, the departure point for some lovely mountain walks.

Al Hamra region

Thirty-five km (21 miles) from Nizwa, turn right at a round-about towards Al Hamra and Al Hoota Cave, both well sign-posted. **Al Hamra** is one of the most elegant and unusual towns in the interior. It has a similar historical timescale to Nizwa, but never constructed defences and thus avoided many of the later conflicts. Curiously, for this rugged part of

Oman, it has an almost Italianate feel, with terraced gardens and a piazza. Many of the grand houses are placed over *falaj* water channels running from the nearby mountains.

Immediately north of Al Hamra is a dramatic twisting road leading to the village of Misfat al Abriyyin, while the road leading west accesses **Wadi Ghul**, beyond which it climbs towards **Jabal Shams** – at 3,009m (9,872ft), the highest point in Oman. The summit is closed, but a track leads out onto the plateau which affords a spectacular view of **Wadi Nakhr**, known as the 'Grand Canyon', an almost vertical 1,000m (3,280ft) drop to the wadi below. Some of the routes into the mountains from Al Hamra are now asphalted, but generally you need a 4x4 to reach the upper mountains or penetrate the old and abandoned villages along wadi beds. Many of these 4x4 tracks now interlink eastwards and continue over the watershed to descend towards Rustaq or Al Awabi.

East of Al Hamra is the **Al Hoota Cave** (Tue–Sun 9am–1pm, 2–6pm; Fri 9am–noon, 2–6pm; last tours depart 1.15pm; charge; www.alhootacave.com). Oman is peppered with sinkholes and caves, but this one is truly spectacular, with a forest of stalactites and stalagmites and an underground lake. Enormous effort and expense has gone into creating the walkways to access this natural cave interior without affecting the delicate ecosystem. At viewing places throughout the 40-minute visit, guides explain various aspects and facts about the cave, such as the presence of long-tailed bats, Hoota spiders and blind fish. Artificial lights illuminate the

Al Hoota Cave

pathway and highlight the amazing calcified structures. Booking in advance is strongly advised, as numbers are limited for this popular excursion, especially at weekends.

About 4km (2½ miles) from the cave, on the road towards Al Hamra, is a right turn signposted 'Balad Sayt 36km' and 'Al Hoota Rest House'. Follow this new asphalt road up the side of Jabal al Akhdar to reach the remote hotel after 22km (13 miles). The sealed road ends a few minutes later at the magnificent viewpoint of **Sharaf al Alameyn** on the central ridge at a height of exactly 2,000m (6,560ft) above sea level. A gravel road continues down the other side to the beautiful mountain villages of Hat and Balad Sayt set within lush palm plantations, but a 4x4 is needed to continue into the spectacular Wadi Bani Awf and exit onto the Nakhal–Rustaq road

The small town of **Bahla**, 40km (25 miles) west of Nizwa, is dominated by an enormous fort which was in a dangerous

Bahla potter at work

ly dilapidated state when given Unesco World Heritage status in 1987. It is a fine example of a fortified oasis settlement fed by water channels, which reached the height of its importance between the 12th and 15th centuries as capital of the Bani Nebhan tribe and centre of Ibadism *(see page 13)*. After more than 20 years, restoration is still ongoing, and it is unclear when it will reopen.

Magic fingers

It is said that the potters of Bahla are born with magic fingers. The clay they use comes from the wadi floor, but to make it soft enough to be shaped on the wheel, it must first be trampled on. When it is sufficiently pliable, the potter then works his magic, fashioning the clay into fine pots and vessels that grace homes all over Oman.

Bahla pottery is renowned throughout the region, and there are several potteries among the plantations and houses on the outskirts of town, where you can stop and watch the whole mesmerising process from treading the clay, throwing the pot (some potters still use a traditional kick wheel) and stacking the kiln to decorating.

Just 10km (6 miles) from Bahla is the splendidly isolated **Jabrin Fort** (Sat–Thur 9am–4pm, Fri 8–11am; charge), built in 1671. Despite the imposing battlements, Jabrin was not a fort but a retreat for the imams, as well as a seat of learning for students of Islamic jurisprudence, medicine and astrology. In the high-ceilinged rooms with Moghul-style arches are traces of what must have been a lavishly decorated palace. Swirling Islamic inscriptions are delicately cut into the plaster walls, and the wooden ceiling beams are beautifully decorated. In contrast to the splendour are the small, plain cells used by students. Below is an interesting storeroom for dates with ridged flooring that allows the dates to self-crush under their own weight into juice. Views across the open landscape from the upper towers are wonderful.

Bat Tombs

Ibri and Bat

Ninety km (55 miles) further west is **Ibri**, a small strategic trading town midway between Muscat and Abu Dhabi. To visit the ancient necropolis of Bat, another Unesco-listed site, turn right at the central roundabout signposted 'Diriz'. After 6km (4 miles), turn right towards Bat, immediately left at the mini roundabout, then right again towards Wahrah. Ten km (6 miles) on, turn left onto a graded track signposted 'Wadi al Ayn 23km'. After another 2km (1¼ miles), the track swings right before a fenced area, inside which lie the 4,000-year-old

5 ▶ **Bat Tombs** (always open). Some are in a better condition than others, but all originally had domed roofs. Most are constructed with an internal central wall, creating two semicircular tombs, each accessed by its own small triangular doorway. At the end of the fence across the road in a walled compound, there is a much larger communal tomb. The graded road continues 20km (12 miles) to Wadi al Ayn, where a series of remarkable stone 'beehive' tombs runs along a hill ridge.

The road between Ibri and the UAE border at Buraymi/Al Ain passes through As Sunaynah, the heart of Oman's oil industry. But to continue to Sohar, a section of road passes through the UAE, which means leaving Oman and the subsequent purchase of a new visa when re-entering.

SOHAR AND BATINAH COAST

The Batinah coast runs from Muscat along the foot of the Western Hajar Mountains, arcing north towards the Musandam peninsula. Many wadis and natural springs keep this flat and fertile area well watered, creating an almost continuous series of attractive ancient and modern coastal settlements. A fast dual carriageway runs parallel to the coast to Sohar, the administrative capital of the Batinah. But for an interesting detour, take the road that loops around the foot of the mountains to visit Nakhal and Rustaq forts.

Batinah coast

The coast road north of Muscat passes Muscat International Airport, official gateway to Oman, and the fairly unremarkable town of Seeb, home of the Sultan Qaboos University. The next coastal town of significance, 80km (50 miles) from Muscat, is **Barka**. It has a fine, stout fort (Sun–Thur 8.30am–2.30pm; charge) with a tower for panoramic views, but has become more famous for the gentle local version of **bullfighting** (bulls are pitted against bulls, but suffer little or no injury) held on Friday afternoons in the winter months. Nearby is the impressive four-storey **Bait Na'aman Castle** (Sat–Wed 9am–1.30pm; charge), featuring both round and square towers. Now fully restored and furnished, this former residence of a wealthy merchant gives a great impression of 18th-century domestic life.

Fisherman at As Suwayq

The Barka roundabout on the Sohar road is also the start of the Rustaq loop, a tarmac road connecting the forts of Rustaq and Nakhal, providing many access routes into dramatic mountain gorges for exciting treks and off-road driving in a 4x4.

Crowning a spur at the wadi's head, some 32km (20 miles) from the Sohar road, the awesome **Nakhal Fort** (Sat–Thur 9am–4pm, Fri 8–11am; charge) is certainly a major highlight. Soaring to a height of 30m (98ft) above ground level, its foundations are believed to pre-date Islam, though the fort itself has been remodelled many times since. Nakhal was entirely self-contained, with well-water and storage rooms for stockpiling in the event of a siege. The *wali* (governor) lived on the mezzanine level in winter and on the breezy upper terrace during the hot summer months. His *majlis* (audience room) is lined with hand-woven carpets, and the harem is spread with carpets and cushions. A sweeping panorama of the plantations and mountains can be enjoyed from the top of the fort, while a walk around its base offers impressive views of its great walls and towers.

Ancient inscriptions decorate the ceiling of Nakhal Fort

The 52km (32-mile) road to Rustaq passes the entrances to several spectacular gorges, such as Wadi Sabt (to access Wadi Mistall and the Gubrah Bowl), Wadi Bani Kharus (for Wuqan village and the Sayl Plateau) and Wadi Bani Awf (for the trek through the heart of Jabal Akhdar to the tarmac road above Al Hoota Rest House, *see page 46*). Fortresses protect these access routes, in-

A Batinah coast beach resort

cluding Al Awabi and **Rustaq Fort** (closed for renovation at time of writing, due to reopen late 2011). The biggest fortification in Oman after Bahla, it is built over the site of a spring which gushes around its base. The four huge towers typify Omani defensive architecture. Rustaq's lush date plantations are watered by more than 200 *falaj*, but bursting out of the limestone, about a mile from the town centre, is Ain al Kasfah, a hot spring said to have healing powers. Halfway between Rustaq and rejoining the Sohar road is **Al Hazm Fort** (due to reopen when its new museum is completed), beautifully set amongst palms and *falaj* water channels.

The Rustaq loop rejoins the Sohar road near Al Musanaah. Between Al Musanaah and Barka is **Ras as Sawadi**, a headland with several offshore islands, the nesting ground for thousands of migratory birds. It is a popular site for hiring local boats on late afternoons and at weekends. The spacious As Sawadi Beach Resort offers watersports, including diving, and horse- and camel-riding.

The coast from here to Sohar is dotted with coastal towns, each with its own fort or castle, the pick of them being the seldom-visited **As Suwyq** (Sat–Thur 9am–4pm, Fri 8–11am; charge), one of the best 'coastal-style' defences. It is worthwhile exploring these smaller towns with their compact harbours and beach-side fish markets for a taste of local life.

Sohar

Sohar, the Batinah capital, is a pleasant, prosperous town with clean streets lined with white houses and tropical gardens. For millennia it was the major port and capital of an ancient kingdom known as Magan, which became wealthy through the production and trade of copper from the inland mountains. One of its earliest trading partners was the Mesopotamian city of Ur at the other end of the Arabian Gulf. The fabulous Emporium Persicum near the Strait of Hormuz mentioned in a 5th-century Byzantine text is almost

Sindbad the sailor

Sindbad is one of the main protagonists of the nightly stories spun out by legendary Persian queen Scheherazade to save her own neck, as told in the book of *One Thousand and One Nights*. Although fictional, the tales are based on the real-life adventures recounted and embellished by merchants and seamen for hundreds of years. According to these fantastical stories involving monsters, magic and flights of fancy, Sindbad embarks on a series of voyages, all of which go disastrously wrong. But through cunning and skill, not only does he escape with his life, but he also returns with great wealth…until his next voyage. Although there are many other claims, all Omanis believe that Sindbad originally came from Sohar. His name would appear to have a connection with Sindh (now in Pakistan) with which Sohar was trading. Sindbad's voyage to China was recreated by Tim Severin in a replica craft named *Sohar* (see page 59).

certainly Sohar, home port of Sindbad the Sailor of the *Thousand and One Nights (see box opposite)*. Sohar reached its zenith in the 10th century, when it thrived on trade with Africa and Madagascar. The seaport was absorbed into the Persian kingdom of Hormuz in the 14th century, but following capture by Portugal in 1507 its fortunes began to ebb. By the mid-16th century, shipping from India and Africa discharged in Sur and Aden

Sohar Fort

and local merchants and sea captains moved elsewhere.

Sohar's fortunes have recently revived, thanks to the development of a major new port, factories and oil refineries, making it second only to Muscat in terms of economic importance. The town has an extensive seafront corniche ending at the harbour and the sweeping roof of the new fish market, and new malls now complement the more traditional souqs. The large, whitewashed **Sohar Fort** (Sat–Thur 9am–4pm, Fri 8–11am; charge) at the eastern end of the corniche is the main attraction. A fortress has probably been on this site for over 1,500 years, but most of what is seen today dates from the Portuguese period in the early16th century. Further north are the Sohar Beach Resort and new Butterfly Hotel Suites.

Continuing along the main coastal highway is Shinas, where most of the traffic turns inland on the main road to Dubai, with the border control at Hatta. North along the coast road is the border with Fujairah emirate at Khitmat Milahah, 90km (55 miles) from Sohar.

Wadi Jizzi

The road between Sohar and Buraymi runs inland up **Wadi Jizzi**, a thoroughfare between the mountains used for thousands of years to transport extracted minerals, particularly copper. There are two sites of interest both connected with the ancient copper trade – a ziggurat temple and the Lusayl Arch, both reachable by car.

Three km (2 miles) after leaving the Falaj al Qubail roundabout on the outskirts of Sohar, the brash new Crowne Plaza Hotel is seen on the right. The great belching smokestack of the modern Oman Mining processing plant, 25km (15 miles) on, is always a good location marker when exploring the area. To reach the ziggurat, turn right off the Buraymi road in front of the Oman Mining gates and double back up what appears to be a private road into the copper plant. Follow

Flooded waste pit in the arid Sohar hinterland, where copper has been mined for millennia this public tarmac road between the two halves of the mining plant. After 5km (3 miles) you'll be glad to know that you are not going into Rehab (signposted left) as you take the road fork 1,500m/yds to a fenced area on the left with 'Keep Out' signs, inside which is a huge open-cast mine known as 'Beidha Pit', now disused. Just over a kilometre (⅔ mile) further on is a signpost indicating Beidha village to

Ziggurats

Ziggurats were stepped pyramid temples built from about 2,200BC to 500BC in the Gulf region, of which about 25 survive. The best preserved is at Ur in Iraq, while the largest is at Elam in Iran. Nobody knows for certain how or why these vast temples were built, but it is thought that they were designed as dwelling places for the gods rather than places of worship.

the left, and here on the right, beside the road, are the stone ramps and tiers of the ziggurat.

The small **Arja Ziggurat**, the only such temple yet found in Arabia, reveals the ancient connections with Persia and Mesopotamia, where ziggurats are more common. Many ancient copper-smelting sites have been discovered in the area, some dating back 4,000 years, and it is likely that Sumerian gods would have been worshipped at such a temple. Shaped like a step pyramid with an access ramp up one side, this temple probably had four tiers, of which only the lower two remain. Dating is difficult, but it could be from around 1,000BC.

The **Lusayl Arch** is on the other side of the Buraymi Road, reached by returning to the Oman Mining plant and continuing towards Buraymi. Two km (1¼ miles) after the plant, take the slip road signposted 'Sehaylah al Sharqiyah'. Turn left under the road, signposted 'Oman Mining/Sohar' as if returning back towards Sohar, and instead of rejoining the main road, turn right at the end of the crash barriers onto an old potholed tarmac road. Pass the small labourers' camp

The Lusayl Arch

of Oman Abrasives on the left and cross a wadi bed as the road becomes a gravel track, but still good enough for non-4x4 cars. Enter a large clearing with an abandoned, fenced mine opening on the right. Park here and walk between the dead palm trees on the left and an abandoned white building on the right. Pass the multicoloured flooded waste pits on the left, keeping away from the crumbling and overhanging edges. The Lusayl Arch is 200m/yds ahead on the right. Quite why this small natural arch has been chosen to promote Oman's tourism industry is a mystery. It is pleasant enough, but hardly a major attraction, and it is unclear if visitors are actually permitted to be here, but the unearthly apocalyptic setting produced by millennia of copper mining certainly leaves a lasting impression.

The main road continues to Buraymi, an oasis town of three villages, but greatly undeveloped compared with its six neighbouring villages that now constitute Al Ain, lying within Abu Dhabi emirate. It is possible to visit Buraymi, observe Jabal Hafit and drive south towards the oilfields around As Sunaynah and on to Ibri and Nizwa; however, as the border post is several kilometres before Buraymi, this involves the cancellation of your current visa and the purchase of another one to get back into Oman (even though you've never left Oman). This is regardless of whether you travel onto Nizwa or return to Sohar from Buraymi.

SUR AND THE EAST

One of the most varied regions of the country is the coastal strip between Muscat and Ras al Hadd, the most easterly point in Arabia. Between the desert and the rugged coast around Sur is a range of dramatic mountains, indented with voluminous caves, jagged sinkholes and weathered wadis. The main coastal towns on this stretch are Qurayyat, an important fishing community, and Sur, a historic boatbuilding and trading centre. A two-day circuit runs inland from the east coast back to Muscat through numerous towns along the edge of the spectacular Wahibah sand sea, from where excursions can be taken into the desert.

Building a dhow in Sur shipyard

Muscat to Sur

The modern road from Muscat leaves Ruwi and runs through some narrow gorges before passing Al Amrat and its stargazing observation site, exactly on the Tropic of Cancer. Another 30km (18 miles) on, the road skirts the **Wadi Sireen Reserve**, set up to protect the Arabian tahr, a

The Bimmah Sinkhole

rare breed of mountain goat indigenous to the Hajar Mountains. The road reaches the coast at **Qurayyat**, a town of mangrove swamps, but now being pleasantly developed. The modern coastal highway then slices along the cliffs with many access points into the mountains, the easiest being Wadi al Arbiyeen, some 5km (3 miles) after the toll-booths. Eight km (5 miles) later is a sign to Dibab and the Hawryat Najm Park, the local name for the **Bimmah Sinkhole**. One of several in Oman, the hole is about 70m (230ft) wide and 30m (98ft) deep. It was created when the limestone roof of a cave collapsed. There are changing rooms if you wish to put on your swimming costume and clamber down for a cooling dip in the blue-green water. In the mountains above lies **Majlis al Jinn** ('meeting place of spirits'), one of the largest natural cave chambers in the world.

Beyond the popular camping spot of Fins Beach is the town of **Tiwi**, sandwiched between two dramatic wadis. The first, **Wadi Shab**, offers a great two-hour return walk. A local boat carries walkers across a stretch of water to the start of the walk, which passes through plantations and canyons (you may have to wade through some water, depending on water levels). **Wadi Tiwi**, on the other side of the town, is quite different, as 4x4 vehicles can drive more than 7km (4 miles) along it to the small hamlet of Mibam, beyond which is further easy trekking. The more adventurous can arrange to camp overnight and climb over the mountains to drop into Wadi Bani Khalid on the other side.

A little further down the coast is the once great port of **Qalhat**. When Muslim explorer Ibn Battuta came here in the 14th century he described a city thriving on the trade of horses, but the ancient city was subsequently destroyed by an earthquake and then by Portuguese invaders. Note that some coastal towns are only accessible from the new highway when travelling from the Sur direction. The road into Sur now runs inland past the large liquid natural gas complex run by Oman LNG.

Sur

From Qalhat, the road descends to the port of **Sur**. Famous for its great tradition of boatbuilding, it was a major trading port with East Africa, especially Zanzibar, during the 18th and 19th centuries, but its prosperity declined after

⑪

Recreating Sindbad's voyage

The adventures of Sindbad as recounted in the *One Thousand and One Nights* are almost certainly based on real accounts of ancient Omani mariners. At least 3,000 years ago the monsoon winds allowed them to trade copper and incense beyond India to the Far East. On the way back they carried silk, spices, precious stones, gold and porcelain. Irish adventurer Tim Severin wanted to recreate such epic sea journeys to China, and oversaw the construction of a typical 9th-century boat, built with wooden planks sewn together by coconut-fibre rope. Severin chose the boatbuilding town of Sur to get this type of *boom* constructed in just seven months by a specialist team. The name *Sohar* was chosen, as most Omanis believe that to be the birthplace of Sindbad. On 21 November 1980 Severin's team set sail across the Indian Ocean using 1,000-year-old technology and night stars for navigation. They sailed the maritime silk route past India, Sri Lanka, Sumatra and Malaysia to arrive in Canton less than eight months later.

Fatah al Khair, one of the last ocean-going passenger dhows

slavery was abolished. The recently renovated **Sunaysilah Castle** (Sat–Thur 7am–5pm; free) is over 300 years old. Sitting on a low hill, it offers extensive views over the modern town (the best views are from the western tower, accessed via a wooden rung ladder). The crumbling Old Town is located on a spit of land that is almost an island at the entrance to the shallow lagoon, with the adjoining town of Al Ayjah on the other side. The terrace of the run-down Al Ayjah Bridge restaurant and coffee shop has views to die for, looking out across the end of the lagoon towards a line of whitewashed houses, lighthouse, mosque and moored dhows.

The main sights here are the nearby **boatyards**, with new wooden craft at various stages of completion and the new **Maritime Museum.** Exhibits are still being moved here from the old museum collection near Sunaysilah Castle, but some full-sized boats are on display, including *Fatah al Khair*. This restored ocean-going passenger dhow, known as a *ghanjah*, was one of the last of its kind to be built in Sur about 70 years ago. The new Al Ayjah road bridge towards Ras al Hadd crosses the entrance of the lagoon but is only for smaller vehicles.

It is 34km (21 miles) from Al Ayjah Bridge to a T junction signposting Ras al Hadd to the left and Ras al Jinz to the right. Four km (2½ miles) after turning left is a small round-about, approaching Ras al Hadd. Turn left here for the 7km (4-mile) winding road to Turtle Beach Resort nestled on the edge of Khawr al Hajar lagoon; otherwise continue straight ahead to drive around the other side of the lagoon. The 450-year-old Ras al Hadd Castle is on the left after 6km (3½ miles), and Ras al Hadd Beach Hotel is 3km (2 miles) further on. Between the castle and the hotel are the two runways of the disused RAF base on the expanse of ground to the right.

Turtle-watching

Witnessing the remarkable spectacle of female turtles laying their eggs in the sand south of Ras al Hadd has become one of the highlights for many visitors to Oman. More turtles arrive on the beaches each night during the main laying season between July and October, but they can turn up on any night of the year. There is nothing to stop anyone simply spending the night along any of the beaches outside the Ras al Jinz reserve in the hope of seeing a turtle. But as these green turtles (*Chelonia mydas*) are an endangered

The endangered green turtle

species, the whole idea of the turtle reserve is to protect them from human interference and allow them to lay their eggs in peace. Egg-laying and hatching turtles are only seen at night.

12 ▶   The **Ras al Jinz Turtle Reserve** (9pm and 4.30am; charge; tel: 9655 0606/0/07, www.rasaljinz-turtlereserve.com) was established by royal decree in 1996 and is committed to protecting the sea turtles and their natural environment, and the beach visits are responsibly managed. They are conducted twice nightly: groups of 30 assemble at the reserve to be guided to the beach at 9pm (for the egg-laying) and at 4.30am (for the hatching of baby turtles). Strict guidelines control these visits – smoking, mobile phones and photography are

Turtle tracks in the sand

forbidden. Flashlights can be used to get to the beach, but must be switched off near the turtles. When the guides find a turtle, smaller groups are invited to approach and observe the egg-laying process by low-light torches. From a safe distance the group waits for the turtle to cover the eggs with her flippers. During the wait, the guide explains the life-cycle of the turtles, giving facts and figures. As a bonus for evening visitors, some previously hatched baby turtles might be released to make their way clumsily into the sea. Around 3,500 visitors a month visit the centre, so reservations are essential and can be made up to 12 months ahead. The beach is also open daily for paying visitors from 8am to 1.30pm to observe turtle tracks in the sand, but it is unusual for turtles to be seen in daytime.

As for accommodation, the easiest option is to stay at the reserve centre itself, but there are only 12 rooms, which are booked far ahead. Four km (2½ miles) inland from the reserve is the Al Naseem Tourism Camp, a tented site similar to the more distant Turtle Beach Resort, 22km (13 miles) away. Despite the name, there are no turtles at Turtle Beach Resort, which has a series of wooden cabins set back from the beach of a lagoon, opposite the Ras al Hadd Hotel. Some reserve visitors stay at the hotels in Sur, requiring night drives of at least 45 minutes each way.

> **Turtle facts**
>
> A female green turtle always lays her eggs – up to 100 at a time – on the beach where she herself hatched out. In her 70-or-so-year lifespan, she might return here to nest three times. Only two or three out of every 1,000 turtles born actually survive to maturity. Those that make it to the water will never see their mother again.

The Eastern Hajar Mountains

A circuit of the Eastern Hajar Mountains runs inland from Al Ashkharah and returns to Muscat via Al Kamil, Ibra and Bidbid. Just outside Al Kamil on the inland road to Sur is the As Saleel Nature Park, forested with acacia trees and home to Arabian gazelles and the Omani wild cat. **Wadi Bani Khalid** is an easily accessible series of natural pools which have been popular with both locals and tourists for many years, especially at weekends and holidays. It is a 10-minute walk from the car park up a paved path to reach the pools. Local children will carry heavy picnic hampers in wheelbarrows for a small fee.

Abandoned house, Al Minzafah

Ibra is a modern town with a general souq, but more interesting is the women's souq held on a Wednesday from 6am until noon. On this day, men are banned from trading and the tradeswomen sell bolts of silk and satin brocades, jewellery, sandalwood, kitchen goods, spices and produce.

Just south of Ibra lies the old ruined trading town of **Al Minzafah**, reached by turning left in the centre of town and then right at the end of a long wall, below the first watchtower. This crumbling collection of mud and stone houses, shops, caravanserais and mosques is wonderful to look around.

Wahibah Desert and beyond

Sunset and sunrise provide spectacular photo opportunities of the unique **Wahibah Desert**. Strung along the edge of the orange-coloured sand dunes are the towns of Adam, Sinaw, Al Mudaybi, Bidiyyah and Al Mintirib. **Bidiyyah** has a small private museum (9am–1pm, 2–7pm; charge; tel: 9935 0757) focusing on desert traditions, and **Al Mintirib** has a fort (Sat–Thur 9am–4pm, Fri 8–11am; charge). Many tour agencies have camps nearby *(see page 123)*, from where they organise 4x4 (and sometimes camel) safaris into the dunes, with at least one night spent camping amid the silent expanse of sand and stars.

Knowledgeable desert guides can lead vehicles through the Wahibah Desert to the coast at Barr al Hikman and Shanna, for the regular ferry across to **Masirah Island**, where many of the beaches are also favoured by nesting turtles, mainly loggerheads. Shanna can also be reached on a good, fast road from Muscat in about five hours. The ferry leaves when full and operates a few times through the day; it charges per vehicle, not per passenger. Coral reefs, shipwrecks, marine and birdlife, and one of the best windsurfing sites in the world are among the many reasons to visit Masirah, a wonderfully remote island of beaches, perfect for camping. The one classy hotel and two local ones will soon be joined by many others as this whole area develops.

Back on the mainland, a long coastal route runs south towards Salalah through Duqm, set to become a desert and wildlife tourist hub when the new airport is built. Inland from Duqm is the **Jiddat al Harasis** region and its **Arabian Oryx Sanctuary**, established in 1974. A permit is required

Sand dunes of Wahibah

An unspoilt beach in Dhofar

for a visit, but poaching and increased oil exploration in the area has seen oryx numbers decline, and they are now kept safe in much smaller fenced areas.

SALALAH AND DHOFAR

Dhofar, Oman's southern province, is a ruggedly beautiful region with a rich history rooted in the ancient frankincense trade. Cut off from the rest of the country by the southeastern corner of the Empty Quarter desert, it shares a border with Yemen to the south and in the north melts into the gravel plains of the Jiddat al Harasis. Its mountains attract the *khareef* (southwest monsoon) blowing off the Indian Ocean, and, unusually, the busiest season is midsummer, as visitors come here to enjoy the cooling rains, when the rest of the country is paralysingly hot. Lush woodland is sustained by the rainfall, and along the luxuriant coastline coconut trees bend over pure white beaches. Sightseeing of the region can only be done by arranging a local tour, hiring a taxi for the day or renting a car.

Salalah city

Most people travel to Dhofar by air, a spectacular 90-minute flight across the Wahibah Sands from Muscat. On the approach to **Salalah** the brown terrain is flecked with green, and the drop down onto the coastal plain is sudden and exciting. The airport is near to the centre, reached by a connecting road to the 'clock tower' roundabout, overlooked by the Haffa House Hotel. Immediately behind the Haffa House Hotel on Al Matar Street is a remarkable site within a small, well-tended garden, signposted as the **Mausoleum of Nabi Umran**. Inside a long building is the tomb of this pre-Islamic prophet, almost 40m (130ft) in length, adorned by bright rugs and bouquets of flowers. Further down Al Matar Street is the beautiful **Wazir Shanfari Mosque**, built in 1995.

The centre of the modern city is set around the junction of 23rd July Street and An Nahdah Street, surrounded by regional government buildings and the Sultan Qaboos Mosque. The continuation of An Nahdah Street runs past the gold and silver souq to the Palace of Sultan Qaboos, known as Al Hosn. Though out of bounds, it is a useful marker for getting to the **Alafa Souq** just to the east. All tourist groups are brought here to buy frankincense at a series of shops, each burning small amounts of the aromatic gum resin.

Mausoleum of Nabi Umran

Salalah lies on a superb beach extending 39km (24 miles) east to Taqah. The corniche runs for 3km (2 miles) to the Al Balid district and is a wonderful place to visit towards sunset, when the locals promenade along the seafront or chat in groups at the many local cafés and restaurants.

One of the most important recent developments is the uncovering of the **Al Balid archaeological site** of ancient Salalah. Known as Zafar, it was visited by the 14th-century traveller Ibn Battuta, who noted its many mosques and observed that its people traded in frankincense, horses and fish-oil with merchants from India. This large site of excavated buildings amidst tranquil canals and lagoons is also home to the new and impressive **Museum of the Frankincense Land** (Sun–Wed 8am–2pm, 4–8pm, Thur–Fri 4–8pm; charge, no photography inside; www.gaiaheritage.com). The two indoor sections lead from a courtyard with a fine specimen of a frankincense tree at its centre. The History Hall covers prehistory, frankincense, geography, Islam and modern Oman and provides a real insight into the people of the region. The Maritime Hall concentrates on boatbuilding, seamanship,

Frankincense tree

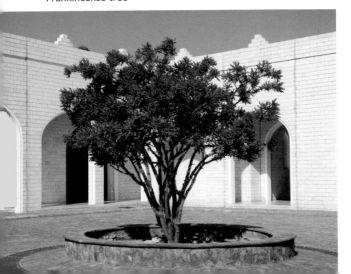

navigation and the trade that made the region wealthy. The site is especially magical in the early evening when it is illuminated.

Salalah is ringed by mountains. Rain falling on these highlands during the summer *khareef* is soaked up and stored in layers of limestone. As well as the great caverns that open up to create sinkholes such as Tawi Atayr, the water is also slowly released throughout the year at a series of springs

Camels grazing at Ain Razat

along the base of the mountains. Known as *ains*, these springs are pleasant spots, all within a 15-minute drive of the coast. The easiest to reach is **Ain Razat**, but Ain Jarziz, Ain Hamran, Ain Tabraq and Ain Athun are all popular evening and weekend retreats. The abundance of open water and vegetation also attracts varied birdlife.

West Salalah

The main road heading into the mountains from the western end of the ring road behind the Hamdan Plaza Hotel is known as the Atin Road. Each side of the road has large areas used during the *khareef* – amusement parks, campsites, and picnic and play areas. Beyond the outer ring road the road climbs into the mountains. Halfway up, a broken cobbled road doubles back on the right to a viewpoint, known as the Atin Cave restaurant. The views across Salalah and the coast are fabulous, especially at sunset. The shallow **Atin Cave** itself is along a paved walkway behind the restaurant, offering great

Mughsayl Beach is known for giant blow holes

views into the neighbouring wooded valley. Ten km (6 miles) beyond Atin Cave is the signposted 'Mausoleum of An Nabi Ayoub' (**Job's Tomb**), another pre-Islamic prophet whose grave is about 4m (13ft) long. Famed in the Old Testament for maintaining his faith in God in spite of the sufferings sent to test him, Job (Ayoub in Arabic) is revered by Muslims as well as Jews and Christians.

Return to the Hamdan Plaza roundabout, turn right and head towards the western suburbs and port area. The Sumhuram Tourist Village and Hilton Resort are along the coast to the left. Eight km (5 miles) after passing the **Port of Salalah** at Raysut, where cruise ships dock, some newly constructed fenced compounds display rows of young frankincense trees. The road then crosses a moonscape desert before dropping down to **Mughsayl Beach**, where white sand stretches to the distant cliffs, edged by more fenced trees – this time coconuts, providing welcome shade for visitors. After the fishing village (a row of smart villas to the right of the road) is an inlet. As the road starts to climb (and opposite a petrol station on the right), turn left, signposted 'Al Marneef Cave', towards the new Mocca café, with stunning terrace views. The cliff path ends at some wooden platforms overlooking the crashing sea, where pummelling seawater has undermined the edges, creating chambers and **blow holes** within the rocks. Hope for rough seas, as the water is forced through small passageways and explodes spectacularly upwards out of the ground. In calm weather, nothing happens apart from a few gurgling noises deep underground.

It is worthwhile continuing further west on the main road, as just over 7km (4 miles) from the petrol station are some wild frankincense trees, just to the right of the road at the bottom of steep downhill bends. These are scraggy specimens which have been well attacked by visitors wishing to draw out the precious white sap. Some hardened beads of aromatic resin might be found on the old, gnarled barks. Even the slivers of wood and bark smell of the wonderful fragrance. Further still are some dramatic views from the mountain road as it snakes up the coastal cliffs, with a few parking places to stop and view. The area of Thaytiniti is rich in fossils of large mammals that used to roam here.

East Salalah

Heading east out of Salalah, there are several turn-offs leading to more *ains* at the foot of the mountains, before turning right for **Taqah**, 36km (22 miles) from Salalah. The town has a thriving fishing industry along the beach, but the main interest is the restored stronghold in the middle of town. **Taqah Fort** (Sat–Thur 9am–4pm, Fri 8–11am; charge), at the entrance to the Old Town, is a fine example of coastal fort architecture, with rooms

Wilfred Thesiger

The great British adventurer made two epic camel rides across the Empty Quarter desert in the 1940s, the first starting in Dhofar. Travelling with Omani tribesmen, his accounts are told in one of the greatest travel books of all time, *Arabian Sands*.

Taqah Fort

wonderfully decorated in period style. Behind the fine carved wooden doors, exhibitions of Dhofari lifestyle, culture and history are well explained in English and Arabic. The views from the top of any of the three square defensive towers are tremendous. The Women's Handicraft shop to the left of the entrance is well worth visiting, with a wide selection of silver rings, bracelets, basketware, incense burners, clothes and hats, mostly made by local women. Just behind the fort, up a steep flight of steps is a smaller fort with even better views across the town. This is around 200 years old and was rebuilt in 2008.

The road inland from Taqah, signposted 'Tawi Atayr' and 'Taiq', leads to two sites of interest. **Wadi Darbat**, to the left, is an area of dense vegetation, camel-grazing and natural caves that really only comes alive during the *khareef* rains, when the waters of the wadi turn into waterfalls that cascade down the valley. The transformation makes it a popular picnic spot in summer. To the right and up into the mountains, the road eventually leads to **Tawi Atayr** (signposted 'Atair Sinkhole'), a large limestone cave with the collapsed roof now lying at the bottom of a huge chasm.

Five km (3 miles) east of Taqah is the entrance to some of Oman's most important historical remains – the Unesco World Heritage site of **Sumhuram** (Sat–Fri 8am–8pm; entry charge per vehicle), once the principal port for the export of frankincense. The trading centre prospered for over 1,000

16 ▶

years thanks largely to the monsoon winds which blew the heavily laden trading boats towards Yemen and the Red Sea. The site is entered through an impressive gateway with some wall blocks inscribed in Sabaean (South Arabian) text. Inside are extensive walled buildings variously identified as a palace, temple, living areas and storage rooms.

Excavated Sumhuram sits on top of a hill overlooking the silted-up natural inlet of **Khawr Rawri**. Once the mouth of the harbour, it is now a freshwater creek, separated from the sea by a sandbank which attracts many migratory bird species, including pelican, stork, spoonbill and flamingo. You can drive or walk to the coast about 2km (1¼ miles) away by taking the track past the **Archaeological Gallery** (same timings as the site; free). This small collection has been superseded by the new Museum of the Frankincense Land in Salalah but has some interesting site finds, showing influences from Marib, the capital of Sheba (in Yemen), and Mesopotamia.

The frankincense trade

Trade in these precious aromatic tree resins, burnt as fumigants, has been in existence for more than 3,000 years. Writing in the 5th century BC, the historian Herodotus tells us that 'Arabia is the only country which produces frankincense and myrrh' to be used extensively by ancient Egyptian priests in temples along the Nile as offerings to the gods. The dried sap from these Dhofar trees was originally carried by ships along the coast to Yemen, where they were repackaged and sent off on the great overland trade route through the Queen of Sheba's territory. Myrrh is a similar but smaller shrub, whose resin was used in the process of mummification. Fragmentation of the South Arabian tribes, the rise of Christianity and the emergence of the overland Silk Road all led to the demise of this once great trade.

Yemen has also influenced Dhofar's modern history, as it was the overspill from the successful campaigns to oust the British from Aden in the 1960s that led to the Dhofar campaign against the ruling Sultan in Muscat. To defeat the rebels, the Sultan called upon British troops and in particular the SAS, in exchange for his continued co-operation with ❼ British oil companies. The coastal town of **Mirbat** further east saw most of the military action, when British forces were often based at the fort which overlooks the town and harbour. To the west of Mirbat is the twin onion-domed white mausoleum of the prophet Bin Ali, set in the corner of a vast Muslim cemetery. His 5m (16ft) long tomb is draped in canopies of green silk.

East of Mirbat is the Marriott Beach Hotel. The dive centre here has recently discovered the wreck of an old steamship about 1,000m (3,280ft) offshore. Running parallel to the coast between Mirbat and Hasik is Jabal Samhan, a nature reserve concerned with the protection of the Arabian leopard and Nubian ibex.

On the main desert road linking Dhofar with Nizwa and 77km (48 miles) inland from Salalah is the desert town of **Thumrayt**, with its large air force base, a survival post on the edge of the Empty Quarter. The ancient city of **Ubar** is said to be located at Shisr, a further 70km (40 miles) north, through a featureless landscape and only reachable by 4x4. These ruins and many others show that large frankincense-trading towns existed in Dhofar throughout the 1st millennium BC.

Girl at Mirbat

Stunning views of Khawr Sham on a Musandam dhow cruise

MUSANDAM

With spectacular mountains plunging into turquoise waters, rocky bays and isolated fishing villages, Musandam is one of the great secrets of Arabia, reckoned by many to be the most beautiful region in Oman. Exploring any part of this remote and rugged peninsula, cut off from the rest of country by part of the UAE, is an adventure whether by land or by sea. Dolphins follow the dhows as they meander through the fjord-like inlets, while eagle-eyed raptors watch the 4x4s as they inch their way up the tortuous mountain bends to see high plateaus, stone houses and ancient rock carvings. Until the early 1990s, the peninsula was a strictly military zone. However, as Oman has gradually opened up to tourism, so has the Musandam, and it has become a popular weekend destination for visitors based in Dubai and Abu Dhabi, just a few hours' drive away.

Getting to Musandam

Getting to the peninsula is an adventure in itself. The easiest and quickest way is to take the hour-long flight on a turbo-prop from Muscat (with departures on most days), which affords spectacular views over the mountains and coast. Slower and less reliable is the twice-weekly ferry. The journey from Muscat to Khasab takes over five hours, but these sailings are sometimes cancelled through the winter months due to rough seas. Driving to Musandam is also an option, but with parts of the UAE in between, all paperwork (including a road pass issued by the Royal Oman Police) and insurance must be pre-arranged. New Oman visas are required for tourists entering Musandam by road and then re-entering Oman on the way back, but are not required if arriving by plane or ferry from Muscat. A departure tax from the UAE might also need to be paid in Dirhams. Some of the minor roads can get washed away in the heavy rains of January and February.

Khasab

18 ▶ The provincial capital, **Khasab**, is a quiet, pleasant town stretching back through palm plantations from the broad harbour 5km (3 miles) up the valley to the airport. Overlooking the seafront is the restored **Khasab Fort** (Sat–Thu 9am–4pm, Fri 8–11am; charge), a splendid stronghold built by the Portuguese in the 17th century. It now houses an ethnographic museum, full of fascinating insights into the lifestyles of the tribes that have made Musandam their home. There

Iranian smugglers

The coast of Iran can be reached in under an hour by fast speedboat from Khasab. Every night hundreds of smugglers load their tiny boats with electronic goods bought in Khasab souq to run the gauntlet of Iranian patrols and supertankers as they race across the Strait of Hormuz.

Zaruqah boat decorated with cowrie shells, Khasab Fort

are interesting exhibits on geological history, fishing techniques and early trade routes, plus a display of traditional Omani boats. This region is the last place in Arabia still to use wooden planks, sewn together with palm-fibre rope in the process of building *battil* and *zaruqah* boats.

Not far away, in the narrow alleys of the wealthy suburb of Al Wusta, is another small fort, refurbished in 2007. **Al Khmazera Fort** (Sat–Thur 8am–4pm; free) has a fully functioning well in the middle of its courtyard and wonderful views from its roof terrace across the plantations and mosque. The main centre of Khasab is set around the new mosque with a limited choice of shops and restaurants.

Scenic coastal drive

The spectacular coast road from Khasab down the north-west coast to Bukha rates as one of the best in Oman. Running parallel with the sea, the road is blasted through the feet of

Snorkelling stop-off
on a dhow cruise

mountains, revealing vivid bands of marbling. Follow the main road west out of Khasab beyond Bassa Beach and the Golden Tulip Hotel and head for **Qada Bay**, a spectacular place known for its petroglyphs (engravings pecked into the rocks). Turn left at the head of the inlet to go through Qada village, always keeping to the left side of the wadi. Just after a large white government building, the tarmac ends. Keep going along the gravel road for another 1km (⅔ mile) to the small settlement of Tawi, surrounded by towering, weathered cliff faces. When the track turns sharp right around an open water pool shaded by three trees, and just before the gorge splits into two, look at the jumble of fallen rocks on the left side. Some of these feature ancient carvings of men riding camels and horses. The location alone is worth the journey. There are abandoned villages on the mountain-tops on both sides of this wadi.

Bukha lies on the Gulf coast side of Musandam. The eastern side of the town contains **Bukha Fort** (Sat–Thur 7.30am–2.30pm, Fri 8–11am; free), which looks different from most Omani forts because of its distinctive pear-shaped tower designed for deflecting cannonballs.

From Bukha to the UAE border at Ras al Khaimah is just a 30-minute drive.

Dhow cruise

The most popular excursion in Musandam is to take a dhow cruise and explore the inlets and bays that punctuate the coastline, often accompanied by dolphins. All hotels and tour agencies offer dhow excursions, catering for between five and 20 passengers. The usual day cruise is spent sailing around the dramatic 20km (12-mile) long **Khawr Sham** fjord to the east of Khasab. The layers of folded rock and geological formations are stunning. With stops for snorkelling at Telegraph Island and Seebi Island, even a novice swimmer can enjoy viewing the colourful fish in completely calm and safe waters, as colourful wrasse and sergeant-majors flit between the more ponderous angel and parrot fish. To protect the local people from too much intrusion, all of the tiny fishing settlements are out of bounds for tourists. Lunch is often a barbecue cooked on board by one of the crew.

The only way to visit the more remote coastal settlements such as Kumzar and Musandam's east coast is to arrange a longer cruise, lasting between two and four days, either camping on the beach or sleeping on the deck of the dhow. Several tour companies offer this as part of their itineraries *(see pages 86 and 123)*. **Kumzar village** is tucked between huge mountain walls. The houses are strung along the lower slopes and look towards Iran, from where the unique language spoken by the villagers originates.

Sailing around the end of the peninsula can be dangerous because of the strong currents. The constant flow of water into the gulf reduces visibility, but the rich

Telegraph Island

This small island became famous as an unpopular posting for British engineers who were laying the first telegraph line between Britain and India. It is said that the expression 'going round the bend' was used to describe the location and boredom.

nutrients support a wealth of marine creatures such as whale sharks, eagle rays and even pods of orcas. Most scuba-dives are 'drift dives' and generally not for the novice. As the only permitted dive operator, the Extra Divers team based at the Golden Tulip Hotel can best monitor and control the diving activity around this pristine marine area.

Mountain tour

Having seen the mountains from the tranquillity of the inlets at sea level, the next step is to venture into them for sweeping vistas across this spectacular landscape from on high. The sensible way is to hire a 4x4, preferably with a knowledgeable driver. A day trip into the mountains will reveal ancient rock art, mountain villages that are still only reachable by donkey, lock houses in situ *(see box below)* and breathtaking views into the fjords and along the east coast. The view of the beautiful **Khawr Najd** fjord (about 24km/15 miles southeast of Khasab) is particularly memorable – from the vantage point a series of hairpin bends lead down to the sea.

The road from Khasab climbs steeply up to the Sayh Plateau. A rare flat piece of land in the otherwise convoluted landscape, it is cultivated with wheat and onions. Across the plateau, the road climbs further towards Jabal Harim (2,087m/ 6,847ft), the highest point in Musandam. The highest drivable point is at 1,687m (5,534ft), directly below the radar station which marks the summit, from where the views are stunning. Just a short walk from the car park are some

Bait al Qufi

These unique stone buildings, or 'lock houses', which are half built underground, have been used as granaries for hundreds of years. Stores of seasonal produce grown in the mountains are locked up for safety when families move down to the coast in the summer months to supplement their diet by catching fish.

The Khawr Najd fjord

ancient petroglyphs showing human figures and animals.

The road descends abruptly, affording views of cavernous wadis, and leads to the coastal town of **Daba**, the southern entry point into Musandam. Still often referred to as Dibba, it is split into three areas of control under Oman, and the emirates of Sharjah and Fujairah. Towards the northern end of the long bay is the Golden Tulip Hotel, and two bays further north is Zighy Bay and its famous Six Senses Luxury Resort.

Midway between the Musandam peninsula and Oman proper, the Omani town of **Madha** is a real oddity. The villagers of this tiny, well-watered enclave elected to join Oman when the peninsula was divided amongst the new entities emerging in the 1960s. Totally surrounded by the emirates of Fujairah, Ras al Khaimah and Sharjah, the main point of interest is a small private museum presenting Madha's unique history. Amazingly, there is an even smaller enclave completely within Madha called Nahwa, which belongs to Sharjah.

WHAT TO DO

Oman offers plenty of activities for young and old, with as much adventure as you can handle. There are some amazing off-road 4x4 drives in the mountains and gorges, and great opportunities for trekking through the mountain wilderness or more gentle hikes along the wadis. Watersport enthusiasts will revel in Oman's enormous coastline, which also offers naturalists some exceptional bird-watching, not to mention the many dive centres which have opened up an amazing, pristine underwater world. Shoppers can bargain for gold, frankincense and myrrh at the colourful souqs and bargain-hunt in bustling malls. At the end of the day there's no shortage of nightlife, with bars, clubs and live music.

SPORTS AND OUTDOOR ACTIVITIES

Oman is trying hard to position itself on the international sporting map, but faces stiff competition from its neighbours attempting the same thing. In 2009 Oman hosted the Football Gulf Cup of Nations, which it won for the first time in its history, defeating Saudi Arabia in the final. In December 2010 it was the venue for the Asian Beach Games, centred on the coastal town of Al Musanaah. The year 2010 also saw the first running of the Tour of Oman professional six-day cycling race, which is hoped to be an annual event.

Scuba-diving. Most beach hotels have a dive centre, a number of which are run by the Extra Divers organisation, www.extra divers.info. These include Salalah, Mirbat, Al Sawadi, Khasab, Zighy Bay and Muscat's established operation at the Oman Dive Centre, www.omandivecenter.com, which has developed

Snorkelling at the Khawr Sham fjord in Musandam

from a few beach cabins in the mid-1990s into a major dive centre with all facilities, including beachside restaurant. Further along the coast is the Shangri-La Barr al Jissah Resort, with its own dive centre, www.euro-divers.com. Most dive boats offer spare places for snorkellers if conditions are suitable.

Desert safaris and off-road driving. The mountains and desert interior of Oman are perfect places for 4x4 adventures. Popular day and weekend excursions give a real taste of the rugged environment, and there are few restrictions on where to go. Nowadays the use of powerful 4x4 vehicles makes this possible for everyone, but there are still risks involved, and every off-road journey should be well equipped and organised. The most popular 4x4 routes are dramatic traverses through the gorges of the Jabal al Akhdar Mountains, such as Wadi Bani Awf, which links Rustaq with Nizwa. The track gets very steep in places and gives access to Snake Canyon for some optional canyoning adventures. Routes and details are available from specific publications such as the excellent *Oman Off-Road* (www.explorerpublishing.com). Visitors can arrange desert expeditions themselves, planning to camp overnight, but local knowledge is invaluable, and there should

Dive sites of Oman

South of Muscat, the popular dive sites at Bandar Khayran boast over 200 species of fish, 40 types of coral and the wreck of the *Al Munassir*, an 84m (275ft) naval ship sunk as an artificial reef. The whole Bandar Khayran area is set for further development as a diving and snorkelling centre. The Daymaniyat Archipelago, 18km (11 miles) off Barka on the Batinah coast, is a protected nature reserve of nine islands, with 20 dive locations easily accessible from the Al Sawadi Beach Resort, www.extra divers.info. More remote dive sites off Salalah, Mirbat and Musandam are almost pristine, but more suited to experienced divers.

Experience the raw beauty of the desert and mountains in a 4x4

always be an experienced person responsible for navigation, communication, equipment and emergency procedures. Never go into the mountains or desert with just a single vehicle. Local tour operators organise desert tours *(see page 123)*.

Walking and trekking. Popular and easy wadi walks include Wadi Shab and Wadi Tawi on the coastal side of the Eastern Hajar Mountains, and Wadi Bani Khalid on the inland side. Some walking trails, such as the C38 trail behind Mutrah *(see page 32)*, were established a few years ago, but signage is unreliable. Even the most gentle trek should be well prepared and equipped. Invest in a good map and always take plenty of water. Many tour companies offer organised walks and treks of varying degrees of difficulty, which are a safer option for the less experienced hiker.

Sailing. Windy conditions for most of the year make sailing a popular pastime. For details of tuition, events and races, contact the Ras al Hamra Boat Club, tel: 2467 8759, www.rahbc.pdorc.com, which has Hobie Cats and Laser dinghies, as well as Optimists and Toppers for younger members. The Boat Club also offers diving, fishing, kayaking and powerboating. Sailboats, kayaks and canoes are available at the Al Bustan Palace Hotel and other beach resorts.

Watersports. The long coastline offers excellent opportunities for watersports from windsurfing, kitesurfing and wakeboarding to water-skiing and jet-skiing. With almost constant winds, kitesurfing is extremely popular. At Az Zaibah Beach, near Muscat, a six-hour beginner course is run by Kitesurfing Lessons, tel: 9400 6007, www.kitesurfing lessons.com. Jet skis can be hired by the hour at the As Sawadi Beach Resort.

Jet-skiing near Muscat

Sport fishing. Most large tour operators can organise deep-sea fishing excursions *(see page 123)*, but there are several specialists, including Sidab Sea Tours, tel: 9946 1834, www.sidabseatours. com, which also offer dolphin-watching and snorkelling trips. Or try the fishing section of the Ras al Hamra Boat Club, www.fishing. pdorc.com. Some hotels, such as the Hilton Resort in Salalah, also offer game fishing. Commonly caught fish include yellow-fin tuna, sailfish and barracuda.

Dhow cruises. Sidab Sea Tours, tel: 9946 1834, www. sidabseatours.com, and Al-

sansool Sea Tours, tel: 9274
8669, www.alsansool.net,
both operate dhow cruises
from Mutrah harbour, as
well as snorkelling and
dolphin-watching trips.

Semi-submersible. The *Al
Khayran*, tel: 2473 7288 ext
200 or 9210 8901, www.
alkhayran.com, is a semi-
submersible craft that takes
up to 28 passengers on an
'underwater tour' to observe

Sanaw camel market

the coral reefs and marine life. Tours leave Marina Bandar
al Rowdha daily at 9am, 10.30am, 1pm and 2.30pm and
transfer to Bandar Khayran, where the semi-sub is stationed.

Swimming and public beaches. Many resort hotels, such as
the Al Bustan Palace and Crowne Plaza Muscat, have long
stretches of white sandy beach within safe lagoons or sheltered
bays that are ideal for swimming. But there are also good public beaches in the centre of many major towns such as Sur,
Sohar and Khasab, with picnic spots, shade awnings, showers
and toilet facilities. Note that for safety reasons swimming is
not permitted along the Salalah beaches during summer
months due to the rough *khareef* weather. In accordance with
Islamic tradition, all beach visitors should be modestly dressed.

Horse- and camel-riding. The most central horse-riding
school in Muscat is the Qurm Equestrian Riding School,
next to Qurm Natural Park (Sat–Wed 5–9pm, Thur 9–
11am; tel: 9942 2401). It has over 40 horses for both novice
and experienced riders, and a 90-minute ride includes access to the beach. Private lessons can be arranged through
Muhammad, tel: 9983 2199. Their new centre at Barka offers more extensive half-day horse treks. Horse and camel

Ali al Habsi

The most famous Omani sportsman is football goalkeeper Ali al Habsi, who has represented Oman since 2002. He became the first Omani player in the English Premier League when he signed for Bolton Wanderers in 2006.

rides along the beach and coastal plains depart from the Al Sawadi Beach Resort (7am–1pm, 2–6pm; tel: 2679 5535 or 9953 7661).

Bird-watching. Spring (Mar–May) and Autumn (Aug–Nov) are good times to observe birds migrating between wintering in Africa and summer breeding in Asia. The water pools of the wadis attract herons and kingfishers, and are important resting points for birds flying across Arabia. For listings and more information, visit the Ornithological Society of the Middle East website, www.osme.org.

Golf. Though the sport is not as popular here as in the UAE, golfing facilities have certainly improved in recent years. The new Muscat Hills Golf and Country Club, tel: 2451 0065, www.muscathills.com, is situated on the hillside opposite Muscat International Airport, behind the Golden Tulip Hotel. Opened in 2010, Oman's first championship grass golf course has a clubhouse with restaurant and bar.

Ten-pin bowling. Opposite the Ibis and Muscat Holiday hotels at Al Khuwayr is Oman Bowl, tel: 9857 3929 (10am–2am), with 10 lanes. Al Masa Bowling, tel: 2469 3919, inside the Al Masa Mall at Al Shati, has 16 lanes.

Spectator sports

Football. The most popular sport in Oman is football, even though the national team has yet to make any great inroads at international level. International matches at the National Stadium in the Sultan Qaboos Sports Complex at Bawshar are well attended.

Camel- and horse-racing. Races are usually held on Friday and national holiday mornings during the winter months, but getting advance information can be difficult. The daily newspaper websites sometimes make last-minute announcements. Betting is not permitted.

ENTERTAINMENT

Several venues host concerts and theatrical performances, and will soon be joined by a new Royal Opera House *(see page 90)*. Most of the regular nightlife revolves around bars and night-clubs within the larger hotels, especially at weekends. Some places strictly enforce dress codes, so keep it smart casual. Check listings at hotels, on websites or in local magazines.

Bars and nightclubs. Popular bars in Muscat hotels include Nuts & Bolts at the Al Falaj and Rock Bottom at the Ramee

Barefoot football

Copacabana at the Grand Hyatt

Guestline *(see hotel listings for details)*. Overlooking Qurm Natural Park is the trendy Left Bank lounge bar with terrace and indoor seating, serving cocktails and an à la carte menu, tel: 2469 3699 (below Mumtaz Mahal restaurant). One of the top nightclubs in Muscat is the Copacabana at the Grand Hyatt, whose nautically themed John Barry Bar is highly rated. Some bars attract a loyal clientele for their live television sports coverage, especially the English premier leagues in football and rugby, including Duke's Bar at the Crowne Plaza and Churchill's at the Muscat Holiday Hotel. The Sama Terrazza rooftop lounge at the Park Inn is a great place to unwind with a drink and laidback music. Outside of the major hotels, alcohol is not available at many restaurants.

Live music. Regular nightly venues at the main hotels and many hotel bars have live music at least one night a week, mostly rock and pop. The Majan Continental has two music venues – the Arab-themed Oasis Bedouin show and the Russian-flavoured Barrio. The Pub on the eighth floor of the Al Falaj has great views and a lively atmosphere. Opera fans will soon have a new venue at the Royal Opera House, tel: 2469 1364, www.rohmuscat.org. In Salalah there is live music nightly at Whispers Lounge in the Hilton.

Cinemas. Hollywood and Bollywood blockbusters are likely to be playing at the cinemas in Oman. City Cinema has multiple-screen theatres at Al Shati, tel: 2469 2656; Ruwi, tel: 2483 1809; Sohar, tel: 2684 0312; and Sur, tel: 2554 5544. Schedules and online booking at www.citycinema oman.com. Also check www.albahjacinema.net.

Art galleries. The Sayyid Faisal Bin Ali Museum *(see page 38)* hosts art exhibitions loaned from major galleries worldwide. The Omani Society for Fine Arts, tel: 2469 4969, also stages exhibitions and performances. For contemporary art and photography, check out the Bait Muzna Gallery in Old Muscat *(see page 29)*.

SHOPPING

Oman has many opportunities for great-value shopping at its various modern malls (generally Sat–Thur 10am–10pm) and its more traditional souqs such as Mutrah (9am–1pm, 5–9pm). Beyond the airport is City Centre Muscat (Sat–Thur 10am–

A Muscat mall

10pm, Fri 2–10pm; tel: 2455 8888; www.citycentremuscat. com), with 150 stores, including a Carrefour hypermarket (9am–midnight) and more than 20 eateries. The smaller Qurm City Centre (Sat–Thur 10am–10pm, Fri 2–10pm; tel: 2447 0700; www.qurumcitycentre.com) also has a Carrefour hypermarket (9am–midnight) and 75 outlets. Try independent shops for more unusual souvenirs, such as wedding jewellery, metal coffee pots and traditional Omani *khanjar* daggers.

Gold and silver. Mutrah Souq *(see page 33)* is the obvious choice, where gold is sold according to its price that day, with a consideration for the workmanship involved. Salalah has a gold and silver souq just south of the Sultan Qaboos Mosque. Large gold retailers include Gallery Argan, www. galleryargan.com, and Damas, www.damasjewel.com, both with several outlets around Muscat.

Perfume. As well as taking back some frankincense and myrrh, a unique gift from Oman would be the locally produced Amouage perfume, based on ancient aromatics. There are several outlets, including one in the departure lounge at Muscat Airport, but a visit to the Amouage Perfumery at the start of the Nizwa highway is great for sampling the choices *(see page 40)*.

Artwork. For high-quality gifts, look around Bait Muzna Gallery (9.30am– 7pm; free; tel: 2473 9204; www.baitmuznagallery.com), which offers Oman-inspired original artwork and limited-edition prints by leading contemporary and international artists. It also stocks a fine range of hand-screened textiles, soft cotton-blend

Bargaining

Even if you don't like haggling over prices, it is all part of the buying process in smaller independent shops, especially for jewellery, carpets and souvenirs. As a rule, try to settle for about half the initial price, or get something extra for free. Prices in shopping malls are fixed.

Shopping for carpets at Mutrah Souq

scarves, stoneware pottery, framed photographs, jewellery and cards. Another good source of arty items is Al Madina Art Gallery, tel: 2469 1380 at 145/6 Al Inshirah Street, Madinat As Sultan Qaboos.

Books and publications. Some hotel bookshops sell informative tourist books on Oman, but there are few specialist shops for detailed publications of the region. The two branches of WH Smith at Muscat International Airport have a good selection at arrivals and departures. The branches of Borders at City Centre Muscat, tel: 2455 8089, and Qurm City Centre Malls, tel: 2447 0491, both have good travel book and map sections. Along Mutrah Corniche try Al Marifah Bookshop, tel: 2471 3607, beside Naseem Hotel. Just down the street from the entrance to Nizwa Fort is the Abi al Fadhal bookshop, selling many Oman books and maps.

Local art, craft and antiques. In Muscat, visit the Omani Heritage Gallery (Sat–Thur 10am–8pm; tel: 2469 6974;

www.omaniheritage.com), located beside D'Arcy's Kitchen in Jawaharat A'Shati Complex. This non-profit organisation sells an upmarket range of locally produced goods including silver, brass, copper, baskets, weaving, pottery, leather, rugs and jewellery. Just outside the entrance to Nizwa Fort, the Omani Craftsman's House, tel: 2451 1451, sells local handi-crafts produced by the Sidab Women's Sewing Group, which supports rural communities. If visiting Taqah Fort near Salalah, step inside the Women's Handicrafts Shop for colourful handmade souvenirs such as silver rings, bracelets, clothes and hats as well as incense, perfumes and henna.

Oman is a very child-friendly, family-oriented country

ACTIVITIES FOR CHILDREN

There are several activities aimed at children in the main centres. Horse- and camel-riding, snorkelling cruises, dolphin-watching and sailing are always popular with families *(details above)*.

Museums. The Children's Museum in Muscat *(see page 36)* is an obvious place to take the kids for entertain-ment and education. There are interactive exhibits to en-thral older children and a play area for smaller children. The Oil & Gas Exhibition Centre *(see page 36)* has lots of hands-on displays and in-teresting explanations of oil production and conservation, though under-12s need permission to enter. At the same venue, the Planetarium has shows in English every Wed at 7pm and Thur at 10am, plus there's a programme of live stargazing events. The Natural History Museum *(see page 38)* has some fossil quizzes aimed at children as well as plenty of stuffed animals, and of course the ever-popular suspended whale

A colourful variety of reef fish can be seen at the Aquarium

skeleton. The Sultan's Armed Forces Museum *(see page 35)* has an outdoor area of tanks, planes, rockets and missiles.

Paintball. As popular with the grown-ups as it is with the kids, Muscat Paintball (minimum 12 years) and Laser Tag (minimum eight years) has an arena near the Children's Museum (3–11pm), tel: 2469 7768. Further out towards Seeb is Paintball Oman, tel: 2454 4007, www.paintball oman.com.

Ice-skating. Ice-skating is the complete antidote to life in the hot city, and Muscat's Ice-Skating Centre *(see page 39)* remains as popular as ever since it first opened in the 1990s. Tuition available.

Aquarium. This small but interesting aquarium is part of the Marine Fisheries and Science Centre at Marina Bander Ar Rawdah *(see page 31)*.

Horse-riding. See Qurm Equestrian Riding School *(page 87)*.

Public parks. Every town and city has shaded public parks, with slides, swings and climbing frames for younger children, which usually open at 4pm, being extremely popular in the late afternoon and evening, when the heat abates.

Calendar of events

January–February The Muscat Festival is a 22-day event celebrating Oman's culture and history with concerts, fashion shows, food festivals, gala dinners, arts events, workshops and lectures accompanied by nightly laser shows and firework displays (www.muscat-festival.com).

February The Tour of Oman six-stage cycling race, which runs along challenging mountain and coastal roads. Muscat International Book Fair.

May Oman Travel Mart at the Oman International Exhibition Centre.

July–August Between 15 July and 31 August, the Salalah Tourism Festival (formerly the Khareef Festival) celebrates the monsoon season, when the southernmost tip of Oman transforms from a dry desert to a lush green carpet. It attracts up to 2 million visitors with music, dancing and parades. A visit to Mughsayl is popular, as the rough seas create large blow holes of exploding sea water (www.salalahfestival.com).

September Muscat Shopping Festival. Shops try to outdo each other with attractive prices, extended opening hours, entertainment, prize draws and free offers. Coincides with the Autumn Trade Fair.

November National Day celebrations on and around the birthday of HM Sultan Qaboos on 18 November.

November–March Camel-racing at various racetracks around the country.

Festivals fixed by Islamic calendar

Al Hijra Islamic New Year

12 Rabiul Awal Birthday of Prophet Muhammad

Lailat al Miraj Prophet Muhammad's Ascension

1 Ramadan Start of the month of Ramadan

Eid al Fitr Celebrates the end of Ramadan for three days

Arafat Day Celebration of Haj pilgrimage

Eid al Adha Commemorates the sacrifice of Abraham (four days)

Check exact dates with tour operators and websites, as they change year by year.

EATING OUT

Oman offers a wide variety of local and international cuisines to meet the demands of the many nationalities living and working here. Menus are a delicious combination of Persian, Middle Eastern, Indian and Far Eastern influences, with some East African flavours thrown into the mix. For thousands of years the *falaj* water system has channelled water from natural springs to irrigate large areas of fertile land, much of it being silt washed down from the mountains. Dates are the main crop of the Batinah plain, but limes, mangoes, bananas and other fruits are also grown, as well as tomatoes, onions and aubergines. The cultivated fields also provide fodder and grazing for livestock and poultry, hence the availability of fresh meat, a rarity in Arabia until recent

A wide variety of produce is grown on the fertile Batinah plain times. Oman's position along the Gulf of Oman and extensive Indian Ocean coastline also assure a plentiful supply of fresh fish and seafood.

WHERE TO EAT

For the best international food from Iran, Europe, China and Japan, head for the specialist restaurants in the hotels. The best Indian and Pakistani food is usually found at smaller restaurants catering for the army of workers from South Asia employed in the main towns of the Sultanate. For the most part African, Egyptian and Omani food is best sampled in local eating places, often without a name, which prepare dishes enjoyed by the local population. Vegetarians are well catered for, with many South Indian and vegetarian restaurants, mostly in the main centres.

Ramadan

The Islamic month of fasting, **Ramadan** throws working hours and mealtimes into disarray, especially outside of the hotels. The vast majority of the population are Muslim and do not eat, drink or smoke during the hours of daylight, but non-Muslims are permitted discreetly to use the restaurants and cafés that remain open within the hotels. Non-Muslims cannot eat, drink or smoke outdoors in public, and the sale of alcohol is severely restricted, even inside some hotels. Immediately after sunset everyone breaks the fast by eating the *iftar* meal. Drinking (water and soft drinks only) and having fun can carry on right through the night. The early-morning meal is the final one before daylight. Additional social events are sometimes organised purely for Ramadan, and it can be an opportunity to sample local food, not otherwise available. Keep an eye out for communal meals offered at cultural, social or sporting centres as part of their special Ramadan activities.

For consistent quality and service, the largest hotels are the most reliable, with prices to match. They employ top chefs who prepare a wide range of international dishes. Independent restaurants run by expats from many nations offer very reasonably priced menus and are great places to sample a vast range of dishes and culinary styles. Some of these smaller independent establishments are now allowed to serve alcohol.

Given the size of Oman, the choice and variety on offer will also depend largely on where you are. Musandam is very near to Iran, so its food has many Persian

Al Bustan hotel chef

influences. In Dhofar, which has links with Africa, you can sample some unforgettable specialities such as hot bread wrapped around cheese and honey. Most ingredients are fresh and sourced from local farms and gardens.

WHEN TO EAT

Breakfast timings in the hotels are quite extensive, roughly between 6.30am and 11am. Some local restaurants open early to serve breakfasts to workers, with some cafés having specialist cuisine from 6am to midday. As most of the offices and companies shut for the afternoon around 1pm, lunch is generally taken between 1.30pm and 3.30pm and is often

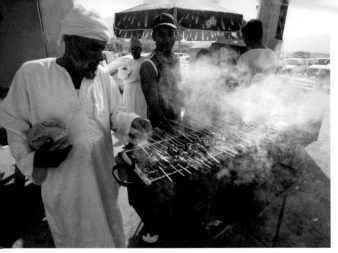

Cooking *mishkak*

the main meal of the day. After lunch, many restaurants close until the evening. Evening meals tend to be taken between 8pm and 10pm, and reservations might be necessary on Thursday and Friday evenings at popular restaurants. Hotels are mindful that Westerners and many tourists prefer to eat earlier, and serve food accordingly. Many clubs and hotels offer Friday deals on inclusive food, buffets or barbecues, which are extremely popular with families at weekends. Most restaurants are very tolerant of children, but few provide special seating or child-friendly menus, so if these are needed it is best to enquire in advance.

WHAT TO EAT

For most visitors, breakfast will be a large buffet laid on by the hotel, usually with a huge choice of breads, pastries, salads, fruit, cold meats and hot dishes made to order by a chef. Often there will be a typical Arab dish, such as *fuul*, made from broad fava beans, ladled out from a large, steaming metal pot. *Fuul* comes in a wide variety of styles and is a popular and filling dish to start the day. *Fuul Medammes* is seasoned with cumin, olive oil, lemon and spices, but there are always plenty of accompaniments to add, such as tomatoes, onions and peppers. A more unusual local Arabian breakfast is *lokhemat* – deep-fried flour and yeast dumplings infused with cardamom and served with sweet lime or date syrup (not for the calorie-conscious!). Many places open early for European-style breakfasts, including several branches of Kargeen Caffe in the central malls.

The internationalisation of Oman in general, and the Greater Muscat area in particular, means that you have a choice of cuisines from around the world. Western-style cafés are widespread, offering great varieties of coffee and comfort food like muffins, pastries and cookies. Outside in the backstreets, especially in Ruwi, Bawshar and Al Khuwayr, are little neighbourhoods that could easily be in Cairo, Beirut, Baghdad or Mumbai, all selling their own types of bread and food to de-

Omani food

A traditional Omani meal depends on your location. Near to the coast, the locals catch plenty of fish and seafood, and have a great tradition of grilling, frying and baking fish, usually with rice. Towards Dhofar, a fried fish and rice dish is known as *Ruz al Mudhroub*. A time-honoured way of using surplus fish is to dry it, and you can still sometimes see salted dried fish on sale at inland souqs. In the mountains, lamb is eaten in various forms, such as *mishkak* – kebabs grilled on open charcoal fires. In the environs of the desert, the staple diet is dates, milk and occasionally camel meat. It would have to be a very special occasion indeed, as camels are far too valuable to be killed just for their meat, as they provide transport, milk and wealth for the entire family.

voted clients. A number of outlets under the name 'Automatic Restaurant' serve wonderful Lebanese dishes quickly and at great value. The 'Arab World' chain has 15 restaurants around the country serving good, reasonably priced Middle Eastern food. Other franchises serve great Indian food at restaurants like Saravanaa Bhavan (South Indian vegetarian) and Copper Chimney (Mumbai), both of which are recommended.

The Arabic convenience foods such as *shawarmas* (giant skewers of meat, often lamb, cooked on a vertical spit, then sliced, topped with *tahina (see opposite)* or yoghurt and salad served in pitta bread), and falafel (deep-fried chickpea balls) make cheap and tasty snacks on the move.

Menus for lunch and dinner tend to be quite similar, starting with a few plates of appetisers or *mezze*, which in themselves can be quite substantial. Originally cuisine from the Levant and in particular Lebanon, these dishes have estab-

Falafel makes for a cheap and tasty snack

lished themselves as universal Arabian food and are very popular around the Middle East. Classic dishes include *hummus*, an international staple made from chickpeas, garlic and oil; *tahina*, a thin paste made from ground sesame seeds with added olive oil and spices; *babaganugh*, mashed aubergine with garlic, lemon juice and oil; and *moutabbal*, made from roast

In coastal areas, fish is the staple diet

aubergines and sesame paste. The *mezze* are usually eaten with fresh oven-baked bread.

A popular lunchtime dish is lamb or chicken *makbous*, where the main ingredient is slowly cooked throughout the morning with onions and saffron rice. Seasoned with spices and lime, vegetables of the season are added, such as tomatoes, green peppers or potatoes.

Main dishes for both lunch and dinner include the Indian-inspired *biryani samakh*, 'fish biryani' – rice, spices, vegetables and seafood all cooked together; *laham mashwee*, 'stuffed lamb' – eaten with bread, but also sometimes made from fish. *Kuftah* are meatball kebabs often rolled up in pitta bread with salad and yoghurt. Many places offer main-meal menus with standard dishes such as grilled meats, fish, kebabs and chicken, served with different varieties of rice, as well as pasta dishes, soups and salads.

An invitation should always be accepted to a wedding or special seasonal celebration, when you might partake of traditional dishes served on a large platter, around which the guests sit on the floor. When instructed by your hosts, just

Baklava, a rich, sweet pastry filled with honey and pistachio nuts

dig in, but make sure to use only the right hand. One such opportunity is at the end of the fasting month of Ramadan, celebrated by *Eid al Fitr*, when everyone is in a joyous mood. One of the favourite meals is *harees*, a kind of porridge made from pieces of meat (usually lamb) and whole wheat. The wheat is cooked in a pot, to which the meat is added and left for another few hours. This mixture is then transferred to an oven (or buried under hot coals if in the desert) and cooked for a few more hours until ready to serve.

Shuwa is the traditional celebratory village meal in Oman when a whole animal (cow, goat, lamb or sometimes a young camel) is roasted in an underground pit for up to two days, until the meat is tender enough to drop from the bone. Herbs, spices and pepper might be added to create a unique flavour. It is usually served on giant platters as chunks of meat lying on a bed of rice and other ingredients, into which everyone digs with their right hands.

True Omani food is hard to find outside the home. The best place to sample authentic Omani dishes is at the more stylish Omani restaurants such as Ubhar *(see page 110)*, where you can sample a delicious *shuwa*, and Kargeen Caffe *(see page 108)*, both in Muscat.

DESSERTS

Halwa is a generic name for dessert or sweetmeats, but it also refers to a special Omani dessert made from eggs, sugar, ghee, nuts, cornflower, rosewater and cardamom. A large number of patisseries and cake shops are spread across Muscat, and many of the sweet, sticky pastries will be familiar from Greece, Turkey or Lebanon. *Baklava* is a light filo pastry stuffed with honey and pistachio nuts. *Kunafa* is similar but made with a more delicate shredded pastry. *Basboosa* is a semolina cake, dripping with syrup and lemon. Omani dates often feature, either as an ingredient in cakes, puddings, rolls or pastry, or more exotically in date ice cream.

DRINKS

Alcohol is served in most major hotels and clubs whose restaurants, bars and nightclubs are often lively establishments, especially at weekends. Coffee shops and cafés are located all over Muscat, serving a wide choice of coffees, snacks and pastries. Locals drink *laban*, salty buttermilk, and yoghurt drinks flavoured with spices and nuts, while date juice is a local speciality.

The communal smoking of a *shisha* (*nargile* or hubble-bubble) water pipe is

Arabic coffee

Local Arabic coffee, known as *qahwa*, is taken thick and strong, often with dates or something sweet like *halwa* to complement the strong and bitter taste.

something that you will see in many pavement and rooftop cafés. The thick, pungent tobacco is usually mixed with other flavours such as molasses or apple. This activity is not confined to old men. It is quite common to see groups of young people of both sexes sharing a *shisha* in one of the open-air beachside restaurants.

TO HELP YOU ORDER...

I am a vegetarian	ana nabatee (male)/ ana nabateeya (female)
please	men fadlak
thank you	shukran
the bill, please	fattoura, men fadlak

MENU READER

ananas	pineapple	khubz	bread
aruz	rice	kibdah	liver
baith	eggs	kuftah	meatballs
baleyan	aubergine	lahm	meat
basal	onions	makaruna	pasta
batata	potato	maya	water
beera	beer	milh	salt
bidun laham	without meat	nabeeth	wine
burtogal	oranges	qahwa	coffee
dajaj	chicken	salata	salad
filfil	pepper	samakh	fish
fuul	beans	samn	butter
gambari/ rubian	prawns/ shrimps	shai	tea
haleeb	milk	shakkar	sugar
hummus	chickpeas	shokalata	chocolate
jeh	watermelon	shorbah	soup
jibna	cheese	tamat	tomatoes
khall	vinegar	toofa	apple
		zaytoun	olives

PLACES TO EAT

Expect to pay the following for a three-course meal for one person:

$$$$ over 25 RO $$ 6–12 RO
$$$ 12–25 RO $ below 6 RO

MUSCAT

Al Boom $$ *Marina Hotel, opposite the fish market, Mutrah Corniche, tel: 2471 3100.* Great views over Mutrah and the harbour from the top-floor terrace of this hotel restaurant, but the balcony is narrow, so outside seating is limited. Good honest Mediterranean and Middle Eastern food, also serving alcohol.

Al Khiran Terrace $$$–$$$$ *Al Bustan Palace Hotel, south of Old Muscat, tel: 2479 9666.* Buffet-style dining throughout the day. Themed cuisines from Europe to the Far East and à la carte choices accompanied by fine wines. Indoor and outdoor dining, overlooking the pristine beach. Very popular.

Al Makan Café $–$$ *Oasis by the Sea, Shati al Qurm, tel: 2440 4200.* Pleasant first-floor café overlooking the sea. Enormous menu selection of regional snacks and light meals. Trendy hangout for sharing a *shisha* with friends at the end of the day. No alcohol. New branch now open beside Muscat City Centre Mall beyond the airport, tel: 2454 5311.

Arab World Restaurant $ *Al Ghubrah, tel: 2449 1734.* Great Middle Eastern dishes brought quickly with good service in a sometimes rushed atmosphere. Many outlets around the country, especially along the major highways.

Automatic Restaurant $ *Qurm, tel: 2456 1500; Shati al Qurm, tel: 2460 5735; Al Khuwayr, tel: 2448 7200; Al Ghubrah, tel: 2449 9981; Seeb, tel: 2442 4343.* Many outlets for this ever-popular chain, serving good-value Lebanese and Middle Eastern food. No alcohol.

Beach Restaurant $$$ $$$$ *Chedi Hotel, Al Khuwayr,* tel: 2452 4400. Superb Far Eastern and European seafood served in a luxurious private beach setting, overlooking the Gulf of Oman. Exclusive and expensive, but ideal for that special meal or memorable occasion.

Copper Chimney $ *Fairtrade House, Mutrah Business District, Ruwi,* tel: 2470 6420. Franchise of the original Mumbai restaurant, providing excellent North Indian food in the middle of the business district. Watch your food being cooked through the windows into the kitchen. No alcohol.

D'Arcy's Kitchen $–$$ *Jawaharat a'Shati Complex,* tel: 2460 0234. Friendly, efficient European-style pavement café serving reasonably priced Western food in a pleasant atmosphere. Popular with both expats and visitors. Open daily, 8.30am–11pm. Next to the Omani Heritage Gallery.

Fisherman's Lodge $$$ *Way 2241, Qurm,* tel: 2456 8790. Fine seafood dining for a dedicated clientele in a tiny restaurant also operating as a fish supplier. Egyptian chef Tarek has 35 years' experience preparing fish in top hotels. Not easy to find, but worth it for the fabulous dishes. From the roundabout near Japengo Café, head inland towards the Qurm Natural Park entrance along Al Qurm Street. At the top of a small hill, turn left into Way 2241. Open 11.30am–4.30pm and 6.30–11pm. No alcohol.

Japengo Café $$–$$$ *Al Shati Street,* tel: 9289 2868. Stunning location for this uber-cool beachside location with UAE origins. Serves traditional Western food, often with an Eastern twist, as well as oriental, Chinese and Japanese sushi dishes. Good wood-fired pizzas. Great place to hang out, especially the upstairs *shisha* terrace. No alcohol.

Kargeen Caffe $–$$ *Madinat as Sultan Qaboos,* tel: 2469 2269. There are now several branches of the Kargeen Caffe around Muscat, but this delightfully laidback 'oasis café' is the original. Sit on cushioned benches under shady trees and choose from a wide range of traditional Omani grills, or Middle Eastern or

Western dishes, accompanied by specialist teas, coffees and mocktails (without alcohol). View current menu at www.kargeencaffe.com.

La Brasserie $$–$$$ *opposite fish market, Mutrah Corniche, tel: 2471 3707.* New 2010 bistro where fish prepared by a French chef is the speciality. Spread over three floors, with stunning views across the harbour from the third-floor terrace. Top-quality French cuisine. No alcohol.

Left Bank $$–$$$ *below Mumtaz Mahal Restaurant, Qurm, tel: 2469 3699.* Lounge-bar dining at its best. Make a reservation for the terrace to watch the sun set over Qurm Natural Park. Very popular for homemade Sunday lunch and Friday Sundowner menu. Extensive wine list and cocktails.

Miabin $$ *Majan Continental, Al Ghubrah Street, tel: 2459 2900.* 24-hour coffee shop and restaurant. Excellent à la carte Indian food for lunch or dinner. Themed evening buffets, with Monday's Indian and Wednesday's Tandoori the best choices.

Mumtaz Mahal Restaurant $$–$$$ *Qurm, tel: 2460 5907.* Distinctive white hilltop building overlooking Qurm Natural Park, just after the Royal Opera House along the main highway. Continually maintains its high quality to justify being the most expensive of all the Indian restaurants in Muscat.

Sama Terrazza $$$ *Park Inn, Al Khuwayr, tel: 2450 7888.* This seventh-floor rooftop lounge is fabulously colourful, with pool, bar, great views and sometimes live music at weekends. Comfortable sofa seats for lounging and drinking or tables for eating. Their 'Seafood Grill @ Sundown' is a popular eat-all-you-can attraction on a Tuesday evening.

Saravanaa Bhavan $ *Hormuz Building, near Ruwi roundabout, tel: 2470 4502.* Franchise of award-winning Tamil Nadu vegetarian restaurants. A varied menu with excellent thali, dosa and biryani. Look no further for the best South Indian food in Muscat. No alcohol.

Shang Thai $$ *beside Shell petrol station, Al Khuwayr, tel: 2448 3083.* Tasty Thai food in a modern setting. Extensive menu with vegetarian and non-vegetarian options. The seafood dishes are particularly good. On first floor above Pizza Express.

Shiraz $$$–$$$$ *Crowne Plaza Hotel, Qurm, tel: 2466 0660.* Authentic Persian cuisine served in an intimate atmosphere with a choice of indoor or terrace dining. Barbecue- and seafood-themed nights. Open for lunch and dinner, with stunning views along the coast at night.

Ubhar $$–$$$ *Bareeq al Shati Mall, tel: 2469 9826.* Top-quality Omani food specialising in a variety of meat dishes. If available, try *shuwa* – beef slowly cooked for 24 hours – or the camel biryani. Open daily noon–3.30pm, 6.30–11pm. Reservations essential for Thursday and Friday. No alcohol. Just east of the new Royal Opera House.

NIZWA

Bahjat al Sham $$ *Al Diyar Hotel, Nizwa, tel: 2541 2402.* Good choice of Lebanese, Arabian and Indian food, especially the *mezze* and grills. Generous portions. Out of Nizwa centre on the way to Muscat.

SOHAR AND BATINAH COAST

Africa Coffee House and Restaurant $–$$ *Butterfly Hotel Suites, Sohar, tel: 2684 4531.* Good choice of fresh seafood and meat dishes with an interesting and unusual African menu featuring such specialities as *ndizi* (cooked green bananas) and *mhogo* (cassava in coconut sauce). Part of the new building next door to the Sohar Beach Resort. No alcohol.

Mediterranean $$$ *Crowne Plaza Hotel, Falaj al Qubail, Sohar, tel: 2685 0850.* Elegant hotel restaurant with good à la carte choice of dishes from Italy, North Africa and around the Mediterranean. Delicious desserts. Excellent service. Open for lunch and dinner.

Mughlai Continental $–$$ *Manam Sohar Hotel Apartments, Sohar, tel: 9405 4333.* Arabic, Chinese, Indian and Mandi cuisine. Great-value buffet lunch daily. On the way into Sohar from the Crowne Plaza Hotel.

Sallan Restaurant and Terrace $$–$$$ *Sohar Beach Hotel, Al Tareef, Sohar, tel: 2684 1111.* Relaxing location for dining through the day, overlooking pool, gardens and sea. Open-air terrace or indoor tables for Arabic, Indian and European cuisine. Dinner served 6–11pm, but light meals are available all day until 3am.

SUR AND THE EAST

Oysters Restaurant $$ *Sur Plaza Hotel, Sur, tel: 2554 3777.* Wide range of cuisines mainly from the Far East, offered both buffet-style and as à la carte menu. Dishes are prepared using local produce. Open breakfast, lunch and dinner.

Turtle Reserve $$ *Ras al Jinz, Sur, tel: 9655 0606/0707.* Three-course set dinner for up to 40 visitors/diners. Also coffee shop with limited menu available through the day. The food is passable, but this is the only suitable choice for eating in the locality. No alcohol.

SALALAH AND DHOFAR

Baalbeck $$ *23rd July Street, Salalah, tel: 2329 8834.* In the heart of central Salalah, this traditional Lebanese restaurant offers a great selection of *mezze*, meats and fish. Always popular. No alcohol.

Darbat Restaurant $$–$$$ *Crowne Plaza Resort, Salalah, tel: 2323 5333.* Situated on a terrace overlooking pools and gardens with views down to the beach. Themed buffet dinner every evening – Thursday Far Eastern, Friday Indian, Saturday Italian, Sunday French, Monday Tex Mex, Tuesday Mediterranean, Wednesday Arabian. The nearby Dolphin restaurant has a seafood buffet every evening.

Husain Bin Thabit $–$$ 23rd July Street, Salalah, tel: 2329 1010. This is the most central of several outlets in Salalah offering a varied menu of Indian, Chinese and Western dishes. Don't be put off by the fast-food-style decor – the food is of high quality and very reasonably priced. Near Aqwad roundabout. No alcohol.

Layali al Faloja $ *Corniche between Al Hosn and Al Balid*. One of the many open-air local grills by the beach. Join the locals for great-value kebabs, fish, seafood, mutton, chicken and breads. No alcohol.

Sheba's $$$ *Hilton Resort, Salalah, tel: 2321 1234*. Classic menus from around the Middle East with Arabian themes and decor. Evenings only, 7.30–10.30pm, smart dress.

MUSANDAM

Al Shamaliah Grill $ *Central Square, Khasab, tel: 2673 0477*. Best local restaurant in town, serving tasty Omani and Indian dishes to visitors and locals alike. Indoor seating which spills out onto the open central square. Does a roaring takeaway service.

Dibba Restaurant $$–$$$ *Golden Tulip Hotel, Khasab, tel: 2673 0777*. Quality food at the top hotel in the area. Specialises in Italian dishes and freshly caught seafood. The best views are from the upper floor of the Cappuccino Lounge, which serves snacks and coffee.

Musandam Restaurant $ *Khasab, tel: 2673 0569*. Rub shoulders with a local tribesman at this central eatery (at the end of the airport runway). Slightly 'fast food', but still produces good local Omani and Indian dishes.

Poolside Restaurant $$ *Khasab Hotel, Khasab, tel: 2673 0267*. Serves a variety of food for visitors during their sightseeing tours around Musandam. Buffet or à la carte seafood choices and popular poolside barbecue. Interior seating if required. Open 7am–11pm.

A–Z TRAVEL TIPS

A summary of practical information

A

ACCOMMODATION (see also list of RECOMMENDED HOTELS)

The standard and quality of hotels in Oman is high, and so are the prices, but there are some bargains to be had in the off-peak (summer) season or at the newer hotels. During the main tourist season (between October and March) it is wise to reserve your accommodation several weeks in advance. Buying an inclusive flight and hotel package is often better value. Walk-in rates are very expensive, so book online for the best deals, either direct with the hotel or through an online travel agency. There is a shortage of hotels in the lower price range, especially around Muscat. Summer is peak season for the Salalah region because of its cooling *khareef* climate. Credit cards are accepted almost everywhere.

hotel	**fonduq/hotel**
how much?	**bi kum?**

AIRPORTS

The main arrivals point is **Muscat International Airport**, also known as Seeb International Airport (code MCT; www.omanairports.com; flight enquiries tel: 2451 9223/9456), 30km (18 miles) from the Old Town of Muscat. Passengers who need to obtain a visa on arrival should follow the signs to the Travelex counter. Exchange any currency to buy the visa in Omani Rials (RO). Two receipts are given; one is needed for immigration. After baggage collection there is an X-ray check and duty free for arrivals. Alcohol can be purchased by non-Muslims.

Car hire is available from the airport, or you can take a taxi. The taxi stand is outside the arrivals hall. For reservations, tel: 2451 8781 or email: taxi@omanairports.com. Fixed rates are displayed in all the major hotels. Journeys into Muscat seldom take more than 40 minutes, except during rush hour.

At **Salalah Airport** (SLL), there is a list of approved taxi fares on a post outside the terminal, essentially 5 RO within the city, and 7 RO to the more distant hotels. At Khasab (KSB) there are no taxis at the airport and all transfers should be pre-arranged.

B

BICYCLE HIRE

Oman's terrain is ideal for off-road mountain biking, and there are some great adventures to be had along the many tracks and trails. Local knowledge is essential for directions and safety. For details of routes and activities, consult www.muscatcyclingclub.com. For bike hire and equipment, go to Oman Bicycle (tel: 9677 3824; www.oman bicycle.com), located between the Ibis Hotel and Muscat Express-way. For pre-arranged tours, take a look at www.gulfleisure.com/mountainbiking.htm. Road cycling is unpopular, as the road network is entirely geared to motor vehicles. Some of the cruise liners rent bikes for easy cycling excursions along Mutrah Corniche.

BOAT HIRE

Hiring a boat privately can be expensive, so one way to get out to sea is to join one of the commercial dhow tours. A popular excursion is from Mutrah, sailing around the headlands of Old Muscat on a late-afternoon/sunset pleasure cruise. There are daily dhow cruises from Khasab to the Musandam fjords. Most scuba-diving trips can usually accommodate non-divers. Other boat trips can be organised locally, such as hiring a local boat near the As Sawadi Beach Resort to sail around the offshore islands *(for more information and recommended tour operators see pages 86 and 123).*

BUDGETING FOR YOUR TRIP

Muscat has good-value flights from some major European airports, but direct flights are more expensive. Hotels can be expensive if not booked in advance or as part of a package. The following prices in RO (Omani Rials) will give you an idea of costs.

Airport transfer. Muscat International Airport to city centre 8 RO.

Car hire. From 10 RO per day *(see opposite)*.

Guides. Hired through tour agencies from 15 RO for half-day.

Hotels. Probably your largest expense, costing 25–250 RO per night *(see listings pages 134–141)*.

Internet cafés. ½–1 RO per hour.

Meals and drinks. Breakfasts are normally included in room rates. Set menu or buffet lunch/dinner in four/five-star hotel 10–20 RO. Set menu or buffet lunch/dinner in local restaurant 3–6 RO. Evening meal in downtown restaurant 8–15 RO. Soft drink/coffee in café 1–2 RO.

Sightseeing. Admission to forts ½–1 RO or attractions 5–10 RO.

Taxis. Trip within Old Muscat, Mutrah or Ruwi (up to 5km/3 miles) 3 RO. Within Greater Muscat (including Muscat International Airport) 10 RO.

C

CAMPING

Spending the night under the stars amid peaceful sand dunes, on a vast stretch of empty beach or up in the mountains, is a popular pastime for many residents, particularly expats, and visitors. It is permissible to camp almost anywhere, and usually the more remote the better. A few official campsites with toilet and washing facilities do exist around the country, though these are often private concerns (such as for turtle-watching) or are fixed camps on the edge of the desert run by large tour operators *(see page 123)*. Camping tours can be organised by desert-safari operators, with all equipment provided. Those spending a night in the open by themselves should take all equipment with them, including mobile phones and GPS (camping equipment is readily available to buy in Oman) and ensure they leave no rubbish behind.

CAR HIRE (see also DRIVING)

Distances between towns can be considerable, and with the lack of public transport, hiring a car is usually a good option. Many companies rent self-drive saloon cars, but if you intend going off-road you must specify a 4x4 vehicle, otherwise you breach rental and insurance agreements. Rental prices and fuel are good value, and it might be cheaper to self-drive than to hire two or three taxis each day. Daily rates start at around 10 RO/day for an economy car, rising to 35 RO/day for a 4x4. The best value is to book and prepay online. Hiring a 4x4 is great for adventure, ideally by those with off-road experience. It's also safer if more than one vehicle takes to the wilds at a time. If you do go it alone, be sure to take all the necessary precautions and be well prepared (plenty of water, extra fuel, a long rope, shovel, spare tyre and jack and base are musts). The cost of hiring a car with a driver for a day, week or month could triple the price, but is less worrisome and worthwhile if you need local knowledge.

To hire a car in Oman you must be at least 25 years of age. An International Driving Permit is better than your national driving licence. Always drive with car-hire documentation and passport for inspection. Major international car-rental companies and some local ones have counters at both Muscat and Salalah airports. Avis, www.avis oman.com, has offices at Muscat International Airport, tel: 2451 0342; downtown, tel: 2440 0888; at Salalah Airport, tel: 2329 3204; and inside the largest hotels. Europcar, www.europcar.com, has offices at both Muscat Airport, tel: 2452 1369, and Salalah Airport, tel: 2329 2276. Thrifty, www.thriftyoman.com, has a 24-hour airport office, tel: 2452 1189, and offices at Ruwi, Al Khuwayr, Qurm, Sohar and Salalah. Hertz is represented by the National Travel and Tourism Agency, www.nttomanhertz.com. There are also several local car-hire companies. Try Mark Rentacar, www.marktoursoman. com/rentacar, with 24-hour car hire from Muscat International Airport and downtown locations, tel: 2478 6885.

CLIMATE

Oman has a subtropical climate characterised by hot days, clear, sunny skies and low annual rainfall. The winter months (Oct–Apr) are very pleasant, even if some light rainfall might occur. Winter daytime temperatures reach 25°C (77°F), with cool nights down to 10°C (50°F). During the summer (May–Sept) it can reach 40°C (104°F) and higher, with hot nights. This is the 'off season'. Along the coast there is also high humidity, which can make summer rather uncomfortable. At altitude in the mountains temperatures are much lower, with occasional snow and freezing temperatures in winter. Rainstorms are irregular, but do occur in winter. Dhofar has its own unique climate in summer, when the *khareef* monsoon brings mists and rain from July to September.

	J	F	M	A	M	J	J	A	S	O	N	D
°C	25	26	29	34	39	40	38	36	36	35	30	27
°F	77	79	85	94	103	104	101	97	97	95	86	80

CLOTHING

Loose-fitting clothes made from cotton or linen are ideal all year round. Tourists should dress conservatively in towns and cities, covering upper arms and legs. Swimwear is acceptable on private beaches and inside resorts, but err on the conservative side, and topless bathing is not permissible. Bring a sunhat, high-factor sunscreen and sunglasses. In winter always carry a fleece or jacket, as winds can be cold in the desert, at sea or at altitude.

Visitors to the Grand Mosque must wear modest, loose clothing with long sleeves and long skirts or trousers, and women should wear a headscarf. Bring comfortable walking shoes or boots for desert and mountain terrain. Top hotels and resorts have dress codes for their restaurants and bars. Smart casual is the norm for any hotel meal or drink.

CRIME AND SAFETY

Oman is generally a very safe country, where common sense will avoid potential problems. Beware of pickpockets in crowded places such as bars, hotels and markets. Do not leave valuables unattended when swimming or in cars. If anything is stolen, report it immediately to a police station and obtain a report for insurance purposes *(see page 121)*. The main safety concern is traffic danger. Omanis are not the most cautious of drivers, so when exploring on foot always use pedestrian crossings and be sure to observe the signs *(see below)*.

D

DRIVING (see also CAR HIRE)

Driving in Oman is on the right. Traffic jams and parking can be a problem in Ruwi and Mutrah on weekdays. The road system is good, but the general standard of driving is poor, and little courtesy is shown by other drivers, so be on your guard, but avoid offending local cultural norms through abusive gestures or language. Watch out for the bus taxis, which stop or pull out with little notice or indication, and be extra vigilant when driving on roads with tight bends. Once away from urban areas, speeds can be frightening, and many cars drive too close. In Dhofar, in particular, be wary of wandering camels. Using a hand-held mobile phone while driving is illegal, and seat belts must be worn. If involved in a traffic accident, you must contact the Royal Oman Police immediately *(see page 121)*.

E

ELECTRICITY

Electricity supply is good and reliable, using 220v–240v/50Hz current, so most European appliances will be fine, but US goods on

110v require a transformer. Sockets are almost all require three pin
UK standard. Some electrical items are imported and sold with
round two-pin plugs, but adaptors are readily available.

EMBASSIES AND CONSULATES

Australia: Embassy in Riyadh, Saudi Arabia, is responsible for
Oman, tel: 00966 (0)1-488 7788.

Canada: Honorary Consulate, Trade Links Building, Building 1738,
Way 2728, Ruwi, Muscat, tel: 2478 8890; email: canconoman84@
yahoo.com; Sat–Wed 8.30am–12.30pm.

Ireland: Honorary Consulate in Muscat, tel: 2470 1282; also
Riyadh, Saudi Arabia, tel: 00966 (0)1-488 1282.

New Zealand: Honorary Consulate in Oman, tel: 2479 5726. Embassy in Riyadh, Saudi Arabia, is responsible for Oman, tel: 00966
(0)1-488 7988; email: info@nzembassy.org.sa.

South Africa: PO Box 231, Way 3017, House 1384, Shati al Qurm,
tel: 2469 4791; www.saembassymuscat.gov.om, email: southae@
omantel.net.om; Sat–Wed 7.30am–3.30pm.

UK: British Embassy, PO Box 185, Mina al Fahal, Muscat, tel: 2460
9000; www.ukinoman.fco.gov.uk; Sun–Thur 7.30am–2.30pm.

US: American Embassy, PO Box 202, Madinat as Sultan Qaboos,
Muscat, tel: 2464 3400; www.oman.usembassy.gov, email: answer
som@state.gov; Sat–Wed 8am–4.30pm.

Oman embassies around the world:

Australia: Consulate General of the Sultanate of Oman, Level 4
Suite 2, St Kilda Road, Melbourne 3004, tel: 03-9820 4096; email:
c.general@oman.org.au; Mon–Fri 9am–4pm.

New Zealand: Honorary Consulate of the Sultanate of Oman,
709D, Remuera Road, Remuera, Auckland 1541, tel: 09-522 4426.

South Africa: Sultanate of Oman Embassy, 42 Nicholson Street, PO
Box 2650, Muckleneuk, Pretoria, tel: 012-346 4429; email: pretoria@
mofa.gov.om; Mon–Fri 9am–3.30pm.

UK (also responsible for Ireland): Sultanate of Oman Embassy, 167 Queen's Gate, London, SW7 5HE, tel: 020-7225 0001; www.omanembassy.org.uk, email: theembassy@omanembassy.org.uk; Mon–Fri 9am–3.30pm. Ireland has an Honorary Consulate of the Sultanate of Oman, 10a Lower Camden Street, Dublin 2, tel: 01-478 2504; Mon–Fri 9am–5.30pm.

US (also responsible for Canada): Sultanate of Oman Embassy, 2535 Belmont Road, NW, Washington DC, 20008, tel: 202-387 1981; email: washington@mofa.gov.om; Mon–Fri 9am–4pm. Canada has an Honorary Consulate of the Sultanate of Oman, tel: 514-288 8644; email: omanconsul@bellnet.ca; Mon–Fri 9am–5pm. Further information can be obtained from the Ministry of Foreign Affairs, www.mofa.gov.om and om.embassyinformation.com.

EMERGENCIES

In an emergency, call the Royal Oman Police (ROP) on 9999 to alert all the emergency services – police, fire or ambulance. If involved in a road accident, you must not leave the scene or remove vehicles until the police have arrived.

ROP Muscat, tel: 2456 0099

ROP Salalah, tel: 2329 0099

ROP Nizwa, tel: 2542 5099

ROP Sur, tel: 2554 0099

ROP Sohar, tel: 2684 0099

ROP Buraymi, tel: 2565 0199

The ROP website, www.rop.gov.om, is in both Arabic and English, and has useful links, telephone numbers and regional information.

G

GAY AND LESBIAN TRAVELLERS

Homosexuality is illegal in Oman, but some couples do have same-sex relationships. Gay and lesbian visitors will encounter few problems as long as they are discreet and cautious about any outward signs of affection towards each other. Local men will often greet each other with kisses and hold hands, but this is not the sign of a gay relationship.

GETTING THERE (see also TOURIST INFORMATION)

By air: Muscat is the hub of the Oman Air network, with flights to European, Asian and Middle Eastern cities, www.omanair.com. Major airlines flying into Muscat International Airport are listed at www.omanairports.com. The other international airport is at Salalah, with links mostly in the Indian subcontinent.

By road: The major land border crossing is with Dubai at Hatta, where visitors are usually processed quickly if vehicle and passenger paperwork is correct. The smaller crossing on the coast with Fujairah emirate is at Khitmat Milahah. The border with Abu Dhabi at Buraymi is now fenced, but there are no problems entering from Al Ain. Two entry points are possible for Musandam – the main road from Ras al Khaymah at Tibat or the more remote border post at Dibba (Daba). There are two entry points from Yemen, at Sarfayt on the coast and Al Mazyunah inland.

By sea: Muscat is a port of call on most weekly cruises around the Gulf and is often a stop-off on longer worldwide itineraries.

GUIDES AND TOURS

Some tourist attractions have their own local guides, such as Al Hoota Cave or the Ras al Jinz Turtle Reserve, but you might want to hire your own personal guide to be with you the whole time. Tour agencies can provide vehicle, driver and guide for any number of days, for 4x4 adventures, trekking, riding and camping, or for your own tailor-made itinerary into the mountains or desert.

Some destinations are hard to find without local knowledge. Sightseeing excursions and adventure safaris operated by tour companies are always accompanied by qualified guides. Recommended are:

Al Azure Tours, Jawaharat A'Shati Complex, Muscat, tel: 2460 2537; www.alazuretours.com. Organise private tours and day trips around Muscat and Oman, using many specialist guides and itineraries. Offer adventurous mountain and coastal trekking and desert tours.

Khasab Tours, PO Box 464, Khasab, Musandam, tel: 2673 0464; www.khasabtours.com. Specialists in organising tours and accommodation in Musandam.

Mark Tours, PO Box 3310, Al Iskan Street, Ruwi, Muscat, tel: 2478 2727; www.marktoursoman.com. Tours, car rental and chauffeur divisions allow full flexibility when organising any tour of Oman.

NTT Oman Tours, PO Box 962, Muscat, tel: 2466 0300; www.ntt omantours.com. Part of the large National Travel & Tourism Company, with many years' experience offering bespoke and group packages and multilingual guides. Many representatives and branches. Agent for Hertz Rent-a-car.

Zahara Tours, PO Box 833, Ruwi, Muscat, tel: 2440 0844; www.zaharatours.com. Respected large tour operator with over 35 years' experience and a vast fleet of new vehicles, offering many itineraries tailor-made to individual needs and interests.

Several companies specialise in desert safaris and have tented camps on the edge of the Wahibah Sands:

Desert Discovery Tours, PO Box 99, Madinat as Sultan Qaboos, Muscat, tel: 2449 3232; www.desert-discovery.com. They offer many itineraries, from half-day to 12-day tours. Owner/operator of Al Naseem Tourism Camp near the Ras al Jinz Turtle Reserve and Al Areesh Desert Camp near Al Qabil. Camps are fenced in and guarded, with accommodation in spacious tents or cabins.

Other desert camps are **Desert Nights**, tel: 9281 8388, www.desertnightscamp.com; **Al Raha**, tel: 9934 3851, www.alraha oman.com; and **1000 Nights Camp**, tel: 9938 7654, www.empty quartertours.com.

H

HEALTH AND MEDICAL CARE

The standard of both government and private healthcare in Oman is generally high, with good medical facilities. Apart from some emergency treatment, all medical costs must be paid for, so comprehensive health insurance is highly recommended. Visitors needing hospital treatment will be sent to private hospitals, as government hospitals are reserved for Omani citizens, unless there are no private options. In Muscat the main hospital for tourist emergencies is the United Medical Muscat Private Hospital, Bawshar Street, Al Khuwayr, Muscat, tel: 2458 3600; www.muscat privatehospital.com.

Stomach upsets are the most common tourist ailment, often due to dehydration, unclean water or change of environment. Excess sun can also cause problems, so always wear a sunhat, sunglasses and use high-factor sunscreen. Drink bottled water and avoid food not freshly cooked.

Bring enough personal medicines with you, but be aware that some regular drugs are restricted (for more information, check www.omanairports.com/customsregulations.asp). For less serious ailments, there are many modern pharmacies for quick, professional advice and medicines. Hotels can always call for an English-speaking doctor or locate an open pharmacy. There is a 24-hour Muscat Pharmacy in Ruwi, tel: 2470 2542, and in Salalah, tel: 2329 1635. A list of duty pharmacies can be found on the Ministry of Health website, www.moh.gov.om.

Vaccinations: Nothing compulsory, but recommended for tetanus, typhoid and hepatitis A and B. Check at www.mdtravelhealth.com.

Help me!	**Saedni!**
Call a doctor	**Ottlub daktour**

L

LANGUAGE

Arabic is the official language across the peninsula, but English is widely understood. Road signs are often in both languages. Large numbers of immigrant workers also speak Urdu, Hindi and other languages of the Indian subcontinent. In the hotels and resorts almost everything is conducted in both Arabic and English. Although English is widely understood, and Arabic is an extremely complex language to master, it always helps to learn a few basic words and phrases.

Some useful Arabic words and phrases:

yes/no	na'am/la
hello/greeting	as-salam aleykum
(response to hello)	wa-aleykum salam
hello/welcome	ahlan wa sahlan/marhaba
OK	tayib
please	min fadlak
thank you	shukran
(response to thank you)	afwan
how are you?	kaef halak?
I am fine	Al-humdullilah
good morning	sabah al-kher
good evening	masa al-kher
goodbye	ma'a salama/fi aman illah
What is your name?	Shuw ismak?
my name is…	ismi…
I do not understand	Mabafahem
Do you speak English?	Tetkallam inglizi?
market	souq
mosque	masjed

MAPS

Maps are available for Old Muscat, Greater Muscat, Salalah and the whole of Oman. Several useful maps are published by the Ministry of Tourism, including *Sultanate of Oman*, *Muscat City*, *Governorate of Dhofar* and *Salalah*. They are free of charge but not that easy to obtain – try the overseas tourist offices or larger tour agencies. The *Sultanate of Oman Map* has useful city and regional maps included and can sometimes be found for sale in travel bookshops and online. Make sure you get the most up-to-date version, currently ISBN 978-994803 4568. Explorer Publishing have several maps, including the useful *Muscat Map*, ISBN: 978-994844 1144.

MEDIA

There are several English-language daily newspapers on sale at petrol stations and shops. The *Oman Daily Observer* has good international coverage and is online at www.omanobserver.com. The *Times of Oman*, www.timesofoman.com, is similar to the *Oman Tribune*, www.omantribune.com. *Muscat Daily* is the fourth English paper and tries to concentrate on local news, but is not yet online. *The Week*, www.theweek.co.om, comes out every Wednesday with good lifestyle information and listings, while *Oman2day* is a monthly lifestyle and leisure magazine with good reviews, information and a useful archive back catalogue on its website, www.omantoday.co.om. *Hi!* is a free weekly listings magazine, and *Black and White* is a free fortnightly magazine covering the arts, lifestyle and current affairs at www.blackandwhiteoman.com.

Most hotels and homes are fitted with satellite receivers and offer hundreds of channels. Sports channels show live events from around the world, including the English Premier League. Oman TV is essentially an Arabic-language station. Radio Sultanate of Oman at 90.4 FM is a mix of music, news and arts. Hi FM is a Western-style pop station at 95.9 FM, www.hifmradio.com. The classical music station Oman Classics is at 97.0 FM in Muscat and 103.2 FM in Salalah. BBC World Service broadcasting in English is on medium wave.

MONEY

The Omani Rial (indicated as RO or OR) can be purchased overseas and brought into the country. One Rial is split into 1,000 Baisa, so that 1½ RO will often be written as 1,500. Currency notes are 50, 20, 10, 5, 1, ½ RO, 200 and 100 Baisa, below which are coins for 50, 10 and 5 Baisa. The currency is linked to the US dollar and fluctuates slightly against other major currencies. Credit cards are widely accepted, and there are many ATM machines for withdrawing cash. Most shopping malls have efficient money exchanges, offering good rates, and are open much longer than banks. Hotels usually offer poorer exchange rates. Oman UAE Exchange has 27 outlets, www.omanuaeexchange.com.

OPENING TIMES

Bear in mind that there are no standard opening times and the following are a guideline only. Hours of private-sector businesses vary widely, and most are closed on Friday.

Banks: 8am–1pm, Sat–Wed (some also open late afternoon 4.30–6.30pm); 8am–noon Thur; closed Fri and holidays.

Business: 8am–1pm, 4–7pm, Sun–Thur.

Government offices: 7.30am–2.30pm, Sat–Wed, shorter hours during Ramadan.

Shopping malls: 10am–10pm (or midnight) every day.

Smaller shops: Generally 7am–10pm, but often closed afternoons and Friday morning.

Museums: Current opening times for each museum at www.omantourism.gov.om.

P

PHOTOGRAPHY

Oman offers great opportunities for the keen photographer, with dramatic coastlines, mountains, architecture, bustling markets and friendly locals. Take plenty of memory cards or films, as local supplies are limited to popular types. Always ask before taking photos of people and respect their wishes, especially women. Do not photograph police, airports, harbours, military buildings or army personnel. Digital photo shops can quickly download photographs onto disk and print pictures. For technical help, quality photographic supplies and repairs, contact Paresh Shah at Shah Nagardas Manji & Co., tel: 2470 2772, www.shahnagardas.com, located opposite the bus station in Ruwi.

POLICE

Traffic police enforce zero tolerance for drink-driving. After any accident or incident call the relevant ROP number *(see page 121)*. Reporting a crime or theft can be time-consuming due to the paperwork involved, but you will always be courteously processed through the system.

POST OFFICES

Oman's post offices are generally open Sat–Wed 7am–2pm, Thur 7am–11am, closed Friday and holidays. Main post offices might open longer. All incoming mail is collected from post-office boxes. Stamps can be bought from post offices and some shops, but allow up to two weeks for airmail to reach Europe and the USA.

PUBLIC HOLIDAYS

There are two types of official holidays when government offices and banks are closed, secular (fixed) and religious (variable dates). Islamic dates move forward roughly 11 days every year with the

Islamic calendar, which is a lunar calendar. For most people, Friday is a weekly holiday.

The fixed holidays are:

1 January	New Year's Day
23 July	Renaissance Day
18 November	Oman National Day and HM Sultan Qaboos's birthday (the date of this holiday sometimes changes)

Oman's variable holidays change with the Islamic calendar:

Al Hijra	Islamic New Year
12 Rabiul Awal	Birthday of Prophet Muhammad
Lailat al Miraj	The Prophet Muhammad's ascension
Eid al Fitr	(The Minor Feast) celebrates the end of Ramadan (a few days)
Eid al Adha	(The Grand Feast) commemorates the sacrifice of Abraham (a few days)

PUBLIC TRANSPORT

Taxis: The best way to get around the towns is in an official orange and white taxi. There are fixed prices from the airports, otherwise negotiate and agree the price before getting in. Obtain information about local landmarks, as most taxi drivers have limited knowledge and can struggle to find the right address. Hotels and restaurants can arrange taxis for you.

City minibuses: Minibuses link the major centres and main road intersections around Greater Muscat, but are predominantly used by contract workers.

Intercity buses: The main bus station is in Ruwi centre, from where the Oman National Transport Company operates buses to a number of towns within Oman and one to Dubai. They are twice daily (three on Friday) to Sohar, taking 2½ hours (then on to Buraymi);

twice daily to Sur via Ibra (4½ hours); four daily to Salalah (13 hours); three daily to Dubai (6 hours); twice daily to Nizwa (2½ hours). A daily service also runs overnight from Salalah to Dubai via Nizwa and Buraymi (16 hours). For updated routes and timetables, tel: 2449 2948; www.ontcoman.com.

Ferries: A high-speed ferry service runs between Muscat and Khasab in Musandam twice weekly on Wednesday and Friday, with additional sailings in winter on Monday. Sometimes cancelled due to high seas or bad weather. Check at www.nfcoman.com.

R

RELIGION

Islam is the official religion. Omanis and most imported workers are Muslims, observing Islamic traditions and practices. The branch of Islam for most Omanis is Ibadism, with adherents also in East Africa, Libya, Tunisia and Algeria. Friday is the holy day of the week when the majority of shops and businesses close, at least in the morning. Non-Muslims cannot visit mosques, apart from the Sultan Qaboos Grand Mosque, which encourages everyone to learn more about Islam.

Many non-Muslims work in Oman and are free to worship at their own services. Just across the main road from the Al Falaj Hotel in Ruwi is the Catholic Church of St Peter and St Paul, tel: 2470 1893, with daily English masses at 6am and 7.15pm, and an extra mass on Sunday at 5.30pm. Next door is a Hindu temple.

T

TELEPHONE

The international code for all Oman is +968, and mobile phone coverage is very good. Using your mobile phone (GSM) from overseas can be expensive due to high roaming charges via the local companies Nawras, tel: 9501 1500, www.nawras.co.om, and Omantel, tel: 2424 1999, www.omanmobile.om. Buying a local SIM card (with a local Omani number) is a good idea for cheaper rates. To get a local mobile number, take your phone and passport to any telephone shop and get a 'pay as you go' deal. New provider Friendi Mobile, tel: 9840 0000, www.friendimobile.om, offers attractive low costs and rates. Credit is recharged using scratchcards bought from shops, petrol stations and online. All hotels offer direct-dial international services from your room, but these can be expensive.

TIME ZONES

Oman is four hours ahead of GMT, with no daylight-saving time:

New York	London	**Oman**	Sydney	Auckland
3am	8am	**noon**	5pm	7pm

TIPPING

Service fees are included on receipts at most hotels, restaurants and bars, so any tip is additional. If somebody has done a good job or provided great service then it is usual to offer them a tip – waiters and bar staff (perhaps 10 percent), hotel staff, porters (0.5–1 RO) and attendants at service stations (0.2–0.5 RO). Taxi drivers do not expect a tip.

TOILETS

There is a regular system of public toilets signposted along the main roads and in most towns and cities. It is generally no problem using the toilets of any restaurant, coffee shop, hotel or service station. Carrying tissues or toilet paper is a good idea.

Where is the toilet?	**Wayn al-hammam?**

TOURIST INFORMATION

UK: The Oman Ministry of Tourism representatives in the UK are Representationplus, tel: 020-8877 4524; www.representationplus. co.uk.

Head Office: Ministry of Tourism, PO Box 200, Madinat as Sultan Qaboos, Muscat, tel: 2458 8700; email: info@omantourism. gov.om. Official tourist information at www.omantourism.gov.om. Tourist information call centre, tel: 8007 7799. A small tourist desk sometimes supplies maps and leaflets at arrivals at Muscat International Airport, otherwise try hotels and tour agencies.

VISAS AND ENTRY REQUIREMENTS

To enter Oman, tourist/business visas are required by all nationalities (except other GCC states), and passports must be valid for a minimum of six months. Visitors from European Community countries plus the USA, Canada, Australia and New Zealand can purchase a one-month combined tourist/business visa on arrival at any airport, port or land border, extendable for a further month. For details and fees, see www.omanairports.com/visaonarivals.asp. A one-year multiple-entry visa is also available, but each entry is only valid for 21 days, and passports must be valid for at least 12 months. The 24-hour transit visa for onward flights is free. For a small fee there is also a 72-hour transit visa – a useful way to see the highlights of Muscat between connecting flights. Visa requirements can change, so check with any tour agency or visa specialist such as Travcour, www.travcour.com.

Oman and Dubai operate a common visa facility. This means visitors who already have a valid visa for Dubai do not need to get a separate visa for Oman.

Penalties for attempting to import illegal drugs are severe, and there are also bans on some prescription drugs that might be sold legally in other countries. For more information on banned and restricted materials, check www.omanairports.com/customsregulations.asp.

WEBSITES AND INTERNET CAFÉS

All towns and suburbs have internet cafés, often open after midnight. Internet business centres are found at all hotels, with many rooms and some coffee shops having wifi connections. When noting local web addresses, remember that some are '.om' as well as '.com'. Operating websites in Oman can be difficult due to restrictive bandwidths and slow speeds.

Tourist information:
www.omantourism.gov.om Government tourist website.
www.omanvisitors.com General tourism.
www.omanaccess.com General information.
www.omanet.om Ministry of Information.
www.nizwa.net Nizwa and national information.
www.alloexpat.com/oman_expat_forum Expat community.
www.omaninfo.com Tourist and business information.

Oman information:
www.oman.org Oman Studies Centre, with links to many other sites.
www.oman.org.uk Anglo-Omani Society.
www.al-bab.com/arab/countries/oman.htm Gateway to the Arab world.
www.omanarchaeology.com/english/index.asp Study of Oman's archaeological sites.

Official external sites:
www.fco.gov.uk UK Foreign and Commonwealth Office.
www.ukinoman.fco.gov.uk British Embassy in Oman.
www.britishcouncil.org/me-oman.htm British Council in Oman.
http://rs6.loc.gov/frd/cs/omtoc.html US Library of Congress country study.

Recommended hotels

Oman maintains a high quality of hotels, almost all of which can be recommended. They are expensive compared to other Middle Eastern countries, but comparable to neighbouring Abu Dhabi. There is a lack of good hotels under 25 RO per night, but good smaller hotels are appearing around the country. At the top end are some of the most luxurious hotels in the world, whose rack rates quoted below are often negotiable. When you see an advertised price, check if it includes the 9 percent taxes and 8 percent service charge.

Rates at the same hotel vary throughout the year, and there are amazing discounted deals to be had during the low May–September season (apart from Dhofar), but it can be very hot outside! Better deals or upgrades are possible if you are a member of that hotel's frequent-stay programme, so try to join beforehand. Also enquire about special packages with flight and hotel included or other special offers, such as three-for-two-night deals. For longer stays or as an alternative to hotels there are some serviced apartments. In Dhofar, the appearance of the cooling *khareef* monsoon creates a peak period between June and September, when it is advisable to book well ahead.

Unless stated, all hotels provide restaurants, bar, pool, gift shop, info desk, spa, gym, satellite TV and internet access. The prices below are for a double room, including breakfast and government taxes.

$$$$$	over 150 RO
$$$$	100–150 RO
$$$	60–100 RO
$$	35–60 RO
$	up to 35 RO

MUSCAT

Al Bustan Palace InterContinental $$$$$ *PO Box 1998, Muscat, tel: 2479 9666, www.albustanpalace.com.* The sumptuous Al Bustan helped put Muscat and Oman on the map over 20 years ago, when it was originally built to accommodate official guests of the

Sultan. Beautifully refurbished and with superb facilities, it is regularly voted one of the top hotels in the Middle East. Set in its own bay just outside Muscat.

Al Falaj Hotel $$$ *PO Box 2031, Ruwi, Muscat, tel: 2470 2311, www.omanhotels.com.* One of the oldest hotels in the country, now renewed, the Al Falaj is well located. Ideal for Ruwi, the Central Business District and the National Museum. Lively nightlife, with The Pub, Café des Sports and Nuts & Bolts motoring theme bar, and good sporting facilities. Functional.

Bowshar International $$$ *PO Box 1842, Al Ghubrah Junction, Muscat, tel: 2449 1105, www.bowsharhotel.com.* Affordable three-star hotel, with 38 rooms and a 24-hour restaurant with plenty of other choices and shops nearby. Ideal location between the airport and Ruwi/Mutrah.

Chedi Hotel $$$$$ *PO Box 964, Al Khuwayr, Muscat, tel: 2452 4400, www.ghmluxuryhotels.com/ChediMuscat.htm.* The GHM group, strong in Southeast Asia, has brought more top quality into Muscat with this oasis of peace and tranquillity. A blending of Arabian architecture with Asian design gives it a simple elegance that is incredibly calming. A choice of 60 standard and 52 de luxe rooms, all oozing beach-side style and luxury, with tranquil water features and two pools. As good as it gets.

Coral Hotel $$$ *Shati al Qurm, Muscat, tel: 2469 2121, www. coral-international.com.* The old Best Western Hotel taken over by the Dubai-based Coral chain. Wacky exterior and interior styles add to the colourful nature of this Art Deco-inspired hotel. 32 high-quality rooms, but no pool.

Crowne Plaza $$$$–$$$$$ *PO Box 1445, Qurm, tel: 2466 0660, www.crowneplaza.com.* Fabulous location at the end of Qurm Natural Park beside the sea. Fine dining and buffet restaurants with outdoor terraces overlooking pool and beach. Three bars of which the Sports Bar is popular for TV coverage of sporting events, and live Colombian Dance Band.

Grand Hyatt $$$$$ *PO Box 951, Shati al Qurm, tel: 2464 1234, www.hyatt.com.* Lavish five-star hotel which combines the needs of both business and tourist visitors. Located near the Diplomatic Area, the hotel surrounds its pools and opens out to the sea. Ornately decorated with excellent amenities including gym, beauty salon and watersports. Popular John Barry Bar and Italian restaurant.

L'Espace $$–$$$ *77 Al Ezdehar Street, Al Ghubrah North, Muscat, tel: 2449 2318, www.lespaceoman.com.* Style of boutique guest-house new to Oman in former Abu Naeem House. Only six rooms, each individually furnished and run by Sofia Somji and family. A great new option, overlooking the beach, west of the Chedi Hotel.

Majan Continental $$$ *PO Box 311, Al Ghubrah Street, Muscat, tel: 2459 2900, www.majanhotel.com.* Large 159-room hotel 2km (1¼ miles) from Sultan Qaboos Grand Mosque. Small three-storey block surrounding pool and villas. Fitness suite and spa. Lively nightlife with two nightclubs and bars. Good service and food. Complimentary airport transfer.

Marina Hotel $–$$ *PO Box 500, Mutrah Corniche, tel: 2471 3100, email: marinamt@omantel.net.om.* The best of a string of hotels opposite the fish market. Only 20 rooms, suited to independent travellers. Rooms are on the small side, but there are great views over Mutrah and the harbour from the top-floor Al Boom restaurant and terrace. A good budget option.

Park Inn $$$$ *PO Box 1635, Al Khuwayr, Muscat, tel: 2450 7888, www.parkinn.com/hotel-muscat.* 175 rooms built in 2009 just off the highway running through Al Ghubrah. The seventh-floor Sama Terrazza rooftop lounge is fabulous, with pool, bar, great views and live music, usually at weekends.

Ramee Guestline Hotel $$–$$$ *PO Box 594, Qurm, Muscat, tel: 2456 4443, www.rameehotels.com.* Slightly hidden away, but still near to the beach and Qurm activities. 90 rooms over six floors around a small, shady pool. Great nightlife at the Rock Bottom Café, with nightly live bands and Friday DJ.

NIZWA

Al Diyar Hotel $$–$$$ *PO Box 1166, Nizwa, tel: 2541 2402, www.aldiyarhotel.com*. Large hotel on the outskirts of Nizwa, popular with groups. 60 simple but spacious rooms set around a courtyard with swimming pool and games room. Nothing out of the ordinary, but good value.

Falaj Daris $$$ *PO Box 312, Nizwa, tel: 2541 0500, www.falaj darishotel.com*. Long-established low-rise hotel popular with groups, 4km (2½ miles) from town centre. 55 rooms set around two pools and gardens, with 'Castle Bar' English-style pub and mountain views.

AL HAMRA REGION

Al Hoota Rest House $$ *Jabal al Akhdar, tel: 2453 6376, email: hootaoman@hotmail.com*. Just below Sharaf al Alameyn pass at the top of the Jabal al Akhdar Mountains. 20 simple rooms and some villas; the accommodation is clean and comfortable. The guesthouse is popular with trekking Europeans and 4x4 explorers during the winter months, and with locals escaping the heat in the summer.

Ibri Oasis Hotel $$ *PO Box 387, Ibri, tel: 2568 9955, email: iohotel@omantel.net.om*. Friendly two-star hotel near the stadium 12km (7½ miles) outside the town centre on the main road to Buraymi. 25 large rooms in a spacious hotel with adequate restaurant. No pool, gym or internet.

Jibreen Hotel $$ *Jabrin Road, Bahla, tel: 2536 3340, www. jibreenhotel.com*. Friendly new hotel (opened in 2010), just beyond left turn to Jabrin from Bahla, catering for visitors exploring the Nizwa region. 40 simple rooms and a restaurant in five-floor block. A little overpriced, but well positioned to handle the overflow from crowded Nizwa hotels.

SOHAR

Butterfly Hotel Suites $$–$$$ *PO Box 2452, Sohar, tel: 2684 4531, www.butterflyoman.com.* Part of a small chain of new hotels spread around Oman. 42 one- and two-bedroom suites, some overlooking the sea. Indoor pool with adjoining Africa Coffee House and Restaurant, next door to the Sohar Beach Hotel. Good new option for the area.

Crowne Plaza $$$$–$$$$$ *Falaj al Qubail, PO Box 478, Sohar 332, tel: 2685 0850, www.crowneplaza.com.* Inland from the Falaj al Qubail roundabout on the outskirts of Sohar is the brash new Crowne Plaza hotel, temporary home for many of the expat managers at the new port economic zone. More for business than tourism, this large hotel of 126 rooms is quiet through the day and lively at night. Features a four-lane bowling alley and lively Sports Bar with international TV coverage.

Sohar Beach Hotel $$$ *PO Box 122, Al Tareef, Sohar, tel: 2684 1111, www.swiss-belhotel.com.* Operated by Swiss-Belhotel, this has been the beach resort of choice for almost 20 years, midway between Muscat and Dubai/Abu Dhabi. 45 rooms set around a pleasant open pool area and gardens. Good place to relax in peaceful surroundings with bars, disco and lounge if you wish.

BATINAH COAST

Al Sawadi Beach Resort $$$ *PO Box 747, Barka, tel: 2679 5545, www.alsawadibeach.com.* Spacious beach complex built in 1997, about a 45-minute drive north of Muscat. Good for families and watersports fans. Diving is the main attraction, with the beautiful dive sites of the Daymaniyat Islands just a boat ride away. 100 rooms in a relaxing location, with plenty of activities, but quite expensive for what you get. Breakfast and dinner buffet. Resort website often down, so try going through the hotel dive centre, www.extradivers.info.

SUR AND THE EAST

SUR

Al-Ayjah Plaza $$ *PO Box 221, Al Ayjah, Sur, tel: 2554 4433, www.alayjahplazahotel.com.* New in 2011, about 5km (3 miles) from the centre of Sur, on the road to Ras al Hadd (turn right at roundabout just after bridge). 43 bright, open rooms – request one with a sea view. Good option for visiting Turtle Reserve.

Sur Hotel $ *PO Box 299, Sur, tel: 2554 0090, www.surhotel.net.* 31 rooms completely renewed in original hotel in the centre of the characteristic Old Town. No restaurant but local eateries nearby. Good budget choice.

Sur Plaza $$ *PO Box 908, Sur, tel: 2554 3777, www.omanho tels.com.* Four-storey hotel with 108 rooms on the main road into Sur. Three bars and 'Oysters' restaurant overlooking pool area.

THE EAST COAST

Ras al Hadd Beach Hotel $$ *PO Box 400, Ras al Hadd, tel: 2556 9111, email: surbhtl@omantel.net.om.* Mid-priced hotel in a remote location 60km (37 miles) east of Sur. Beachside location and a good base for turtle-watching.

Ras al Jinz Turtle Reserve $$$ *Ras al Jinz, tel: 9655 0606/0707, www.rasaljinz-turtlereserve.com.* This eco-tourism project provides the best turtle-watching experience. Having a room at the reserve centre guarantees your free places on the guided night visits at 9pm and 4.30am. Only 12 rooms, so book well in advance.

Turtle Beach Resort $$ *PO Box 303, Ras al Hadd, tel: 2554 3400, www.tbroman.com.* Collection of beach-side wooden cabins with open dining 'boat' for buffet meals. Quite expensive for a grade above camping. Across the lagoon is the Ras al Hadd Beach Hotel, which offers better value if you're not the 'outdoor' type. Cash only.

SALALAH AND DHOFAR

Beach Villas $ *PO Box 20, Al Daharix, Salalah 214, tel: 2323 5999, www.beach-villas-salalah.com.* A few hundred metres east of the Crowne Plaza Hotel, this small, family-run hotel is right on the beach. Easy-going atmosphere with small pool and restaurant. Rooms on the front look out to sea. Owners can arrange guides, tours and car rental. Extremely popular, so new block of rooms being added through 2011/12. Quietest period is April to June. Cash only.

Crowne Plaza Resort $$$$–$$$$$ *PO Box 870, Salalah 211, tel: 2323 5333, www.crowneplaza.com/salalah.* Large hotel complex in a superb beachfront location, 5km (3 miles) east along the coast from central Salalah. Choice of three restaurants, and the English-style pub and Al Luban nightclub make it a popular nightspot. The dive centre is run by Extra Divers.

Haffa House Hotel $$ *PO Box 427, Salalah 211, tel: 2329 5444, www.shanfarihotels.com.* Run by the large Shanfari Group. 64 large rooms in tower block above two banks, medical centre and Oman Air office. Well located at the end of the airport road overlooking the Clock Tower roundabout. Shanfari also run the nearby **Samharam Tourist Village $$$** on the beach close to the Hilton Resort.

Hamdan Plaza Hotel $$ *PO Box 2498, Salalah 211, tel: 2321 1024, www.hamdanplazahotel.com.* Large facade above row of shops opposite Lulu hypermarket. On the corner of the main ring road from the airport, and the Itin Road to Job's Tomb. 18-year-old building with 186 rooms, all huge, with big pool and choice of Chinese and international restaurants. Very popular during *khareef* summer season. Small office for Mark Tours.

Hilton Resort $$$$–$$$$$ *PO Box 699, Salalah 211, tel: 2321 1234, www.salalah.hilton.com.* Well-established hotel in a beautiful beach-side location among lush palm groves. The 147 rooms are spread among low-rise buildings, with spacious pool, garden, beach areas and dive centre. Focus for much of the nightly entertainment in Salalah, with choice of six restaurants and bars. The Al Maha terrace restaurant overlooks the pool and gardens, while the open-air Palm Grove boasts a delightful setting by the Indian Ocean.

Salalah Hotel $ *As Suq Street, PO Box 823, Salalah 211, tel: 2329 5626.* Opposite the ONTC bus station, near Central Market in up-town Salalah, with 45 rooms, recently refurbished to a high standard. Signposted from the nearby Sultan Qaboos Mosque. Very good value.

MUSANDAM

Golden Tulip $$$ *PO Box 434, Khasab, tel: 2673 0777, www. goldentulipkhasab.com.* Wonderfully located on a low headland surrounded by the sea. Each of the 60 rooms has its own private terrace or balcony overlooking the sea. Restaurant, lounge, 'Darts Bar' English pub and oriental tent for coffee and *shisha* smoking. Good-quality dive centre and shop run by Extra Divers, who also operate their own villa accommodation **$$**, tel: 2673 0501, email: info@musandamdiving.com, in the town centre, providing free transfers to/from hotel. There is also a Golden Tulip hotel in Daba (or Dibba), the southern entry point to the peninsula.

Khasab Hotel $$ *PO Box 111, Khasab, tel: 2673 0267, www. khasabhotel.net.* Located on the main road south of town beside the airport. 42 rooms in the main building set beside a tree-lined pool. Restaurant open for breakfast, lunch and dinner which can be taken indoors or poolside. Cash only. Offers a variety of boat and diving trips and sightseeing tours, organised through its sister company, Dolphin Tours, www.dolphintour.net.

Six Senses $$$$$ *PO Box 212, Dibba, Musandam, tel: 2673 5555, www.sixsenses.com.* A very secluded, high-end resort set in the picturesque Zighy Bay. The 82 villas are strung in isolated luxury along its own mile-long beach. Fabulous food, Zen spa, and a whole host of facilities, this is the perfect place for a romantic hideaway. Only 90 minutes' drive from Dubai – you can even opt to arrive by paraglider.

INDEX

Berlitz pocket guide

Oman

First Edition 2011

Written by Chris Bradley
Series Editor: Tom Stainer

All Rights Reserved
© 2011 Apa Publications (UK) Limited

Printed in China by CTPS

Berlitz Trademark Reg. U.S. Patent Office and other countries. Marca Registrada

Photography credits
AKG Images 15; Chris Bradley/APA 2BL, 2CR, 2T, 3BL, 3BR, 3CR, 3TL, 3TR, 4–5BC, 4BC, 4BL, 4TL, 5BC, 5TL, 6B, 7C, 7T, 8, 11,12,14, 17, 30, 31, 34, 37, 38, 39, 40, 42, 44, 45, 46, 48, 49, 50, 51, 53, 54, 56, 57, 58, 60, 62, 64, 65, 66, 67, 68, 72, 75, 77, 78, 81, 82, 85, 86, 87, 91, 93, 94, 95, 99; Copacabana Club 90; Corbis 18, 21; Kevin Cummins/APA 1, 4TR, 6C, 61, 7B, 24, 26, 28, 33, 36, 69, 70, 74, 89, 97, 100, 103; Elvis John Ferrao 2BR; Fotoseeker 3CL, 61; iStockphoto 5TR, 102; Mary Evans 22; Frank Noon/APA 104; Photolibrary 5BR; Topfoto 23; WFA Images 19

Cover picture: 4Corners Images

Contact us

At Berlitz we strive to keep our guides as accurate and up to date as possible, but if you find anything that has changed, or if you have any suggestions on ways to improve this guide, then we would be delighted to hear from you.

Berlitz Publishing, PO Box 7910, London SE1 1WE, England.
email: berlitz@apaguide.co.uk
www.berlitzpublishing.com